WATER
TO
WINE

SOME OF MY STORY

BRIAN ZAHND

SPELLO PRESS

For the congregation of Word of Life Church and all my companions who have dared to come with me on the great journey of faith

CONTENTS

Chapter 1

Twenty-Two Days

"No one who has ever tasted fine aged wine prefers unaged wine."
—Jesus[1]

"The only wines that actually speak to our whole lives are authentic wines. Confected wines are not designed for human beings; they are designed for 'consumers.' Which do you want to be?"
—Terry Theise[2]

"When we are crushed like grapes, we cannot think of the wine we will become."
—Henri J.M. Nouwen[3]

I was halfway to ninety—midway through life—and I had reached a full-blown crisis. Call it a garden-variety mid-life crisis if you want, but it was something more. You might say it was a theological crisis, though that makes it sound too cerebral. The unease I felt came from a deeper place than a mental file labeled "theology." To borrow some King James style language, my soul was disquieted within me. It was like I was singing over and over the U2 song:

I have climbed the highest mountains
I have run through the fields
Only to be with you
But I still haven't found
What I'm looking for
—U2, "I Still Haven't Found What I'm Looking For"

I was wrestling with the uneasy feeling that the faith I had built my life around was somehow deficient. Not wrong, but lacking. It seemed watery, weak. In my most honest moments I couldn't help but notice that the faith I knew seemed to lack the kind of robust authenticity that made Jesus so fascinating. And I had always been utterly fascinated by Jesus. Jesus wasn't in question but Christianity American style was.

I had become a committed Christian during the Jesus movement of the 1970s when I was still a teenager. I was the high school "Jesus freak" and by the tender age of twenty-two had founded a church—as ridiculous as that sounds now. After a long, slow start, I eventually enjoyed what most would call a "successful ministry." At one point during the 1990s our church was dubbed "one of the twenty fastest growing churches in America"—by those who like to keep score of such things. Yes, I was a bona fide success. *Ta-da!* But by 2003, now in my mid-forties, I had become, what shall I say?…bored, restless, discontent. I was increasingly haunted by thoughts I hardly admitted to myself, thoughts like:

"Is this as good as it gets?"

"What if I just start coasting?"

"Hey, Brian, you've worked hard. Now you can relax, mail it in and take more vacations."

I did my best to keep those thoughts at bay. I didn't want to think that way. I had never conceived of serving Jesus as a career path leading to Easy Street. My motives were pure, but that was not enough to quell the nagging disappointment I felt.

From a certain perspective things couldn't have been better. I had a large church with a large staff supported by a large budget worshiping in a large complex. I was large and in charge! I had it made. But I had become increasingly dissatisfied. I was weary of the tired clichés of bumper-sticker evangelicalism. I was disenchanted by a paper-thin Christianity propped up by cheap certitude. It was safe, but it failed to enchant. I was yearning for something deeper, richer, fuller. Let me say it this way—I was in Cana and the wine had run out. I needed Jesus to perform a miracle.

> I was disenchanted by a paper-thin Christianity propped up by cheap certitude. I was yearning for something deeper, richer, fuller.

Don't misunderstand me, my faith in Jesus never wavered. This was not a "crisis of faith" in that sense. I believed in Jesus! What I knew was that the Jesus I believed in warranted a better Christianity than what I was familiar with. Neither was I looking for a change in vocation—the hallmark of a "mid-life crisis." I never considered being anything other than a pastor. My love of Christ and his church was not in question. I was not "backsliding" or "losing my faith." But I knew there had to be something better than the shallow "success-in-life" charismatic evangelicalism that had been my world for more than twenty years. Like Bilbo Baggins, I felt "thin, sort of stretched, like butter that has been scraped over too much bread."[4] I had been feeling this way ever since the year 2000—the beginning of the third Christian millennium and the onset of my discontent. But now I had reached the point where something had to be done. Like the instinct of deer to lick salt or geese to fly south in winter, I had an animal-like instinct that what I needed was something old, something ancient, something refined. I needed something living that came from the oak barrels of a vintner, not something concocted from the aluminum vats of an industrialist. I was no longer satisfied with the "cutting edge" and "successful." I had lost my appetite for the mass-produced soda-like Christianity of North America. I wanted vintage wine from old vines. I don't know exactly how I knew this, but I knew it.

So, guided as much by instinct as anything else, I began reading the early Church Fathers—those theologians from the first few centuries of the church who shaped Christian theology. I started with Clement and Polycarp and moved on from there. I found Athanasius more relevant than the Christian bestsellers. I resonated with Gregory of Nyssa. I found a kindred soul in Maximus the Confessor. I read Augustine's spiritual autobiography *Confessions* several times in different translations and was deeply moved by it. I was beginning to develop a palate for the aged wine of historic Christianity. As I became acquainted with the beauty of the Great Tradition that had sustained the church for centuries, I realized I had been missing out on something of tremendous value. Eventually I lost my taste for the contemporary, mass-produced grape juice of religious consumerism. It's true what Jesus said, "No one who has ever tasted fine aged wine prefers unaged wine."

By the end of 2003 something had to give. I was discovering the substantive faith of an earlier time, but I wasn't content to merely read about an ancient Christianity. I didn't want to be a historian and I wasn't interested in the fool's errand of trying to recreate the past. I was a twenty-first century pastor and I needed to find out how to live and lead others into a richer Christianity, except I really had no idea of how to go about it. So I did something crazy. In what I regard now as a kind of holy madness I made a desperate bid. I began the first twenty-two days of 2004 in prayer and fasting. I ate nothing during that time. For twenty-two days I did nothing other than pray during the day, sleep at night, and preach at the appointed times. (By the way, I do not recommend this to anyone!) I chose twenty-two days to correspond with the twenty-two chapters in the Book of Revelation. (Did I mention this was crazy?) Each evening for twenty-two days I led a two-hour prayer service with worship musicians in our Upper Room prayer chapel. We would read, sing, chant one chapter from the Book of Revelation and pray prayers inspired from the various visions of the Apocalypse. I know it all sounds very weird, but it's what I did. The evening prayer services were full of energy, but the long days of solitary prayer were a grind. It didn't feel glorious. It felt like death. It *was* death. A long fast is dying. Literally. I wasted away to a paltry 130 pounds. People thought I was sick. I looked sick. I felt so weak. I remember thinking, "I'm dying." And that was more true than I could have known! The whole first half of my life was dying—a half of life characterized by the quest for certitude and success. As Richard Rohr describes it, I was about to "fall upward" into the second half of life. But it wouldn't be easy.

In the middle of my twenty-two day push for a spiritual breakthrough all hell broke loose. Years of relative calm in the church suddenly came to an end. Accusations were made, people got mad, staff resigned, and I was deeply upset. Though I would not have said it, I had secretly assumed God would smile upon my desperate fast, sprinkle some angel dust on me, and I would then peacefully glide into beatific bliss. This did not happen. What happened instead was death. The second half of my twenty-two day fast was pure misery. I was distressed and depressed. When the twenty-two days were over, I didn't feel like I had leaped to a new level, I felt like I had fallen down a flight of stairs. I was bruised and battered. But this much was for sure—things had changed. There would be no going back.

That was a long time ago, but it was a turning point I'll never forget. Now whenever I see the date "2004" on something, I think, "Oh, I remember that year! That was the year that *everything* changed for me!" I quite seriously think of my life as pre- and post-2004. First half and second half. Before and after. Then and now. 2004 is the watershed, the continental divide of my life. It wasn't a pleasant year—it was a painful year—but I wouldn't trade it for anything. *Not for anything!* The beautiful Christianity I have found in the second half of life could not have come into being apart from the pain of 2004. That was the year water began to turn to wine. But wine is not just a symbol of richness, it's also a symbol of blood—and I was bleeding. Often during 2004 I found comfort in Bob Dylan's brilliant song "It's Alright Ma (I'm Only Bleeding)," especially these lines:

> You lose yourself, you reappear
> You suddenly find you got nothing to fear
> Alone you stand with nobody near
> When a trembling distant voice, unclear

Startles your sleeping ears to hear
That somebody thinks they really found you

A question in your nerves is lit
Yet you know there is no answer fit
To satisfy, insure you not to quit
To keep it in your mind and not forget
That it is not he or she or them or it
That you belong to

I once heard an Italian winemaker say that to produce good wine the grapes must struggle, they must suffer. The taste of good wine is the taste of struggle and suffering mellowed into beauty. There's a deep truth there that applies to far more than winemaking—it also applies to the formation of the soul. All the great biographies of the Bible involve suffering. The great souls grown in the Lord's vineyard all know what it is to suffer. American Christianity, on the other hand, is conditioned to avoid suffering at all cost. But what a cost it is! Grape juice Christianity is what is produced by the purveyors of the motivational-seminar, you-can-have-it-all, success-in-life, pop-psychology Christianity. It's a children's drink. It comes with a straw and is served in a little cardboard box. I don't want to drink that anymore. I don't want to serve that anymore. I want the vintage wine. The kind of faith marked by mystery, grace, and authenticity. The kind of Christianity that has the capacity to endlessly fascinate is not produced apart from struggle and suffering. It's the pain of struggle and suffering that confers character and complexity to our faith.

After the first twenty-two days of 2004 I knew I had to move beyond a watered-down, grape-juice faith—the popular schlock I had begun to refer to in the pulpit as "cotton candy Christianity." By August of that pivotal year I had told my church I was packing my bags from the Charismatic Movement and moving on. The congregation applauded. Except neither they nor I really knew what would come next. The problem was I was embarrassingly ignorant of "the good stuff." I had been reading the early Church Fathers, philosophy, and classic literature. Saint Augustine, Søren Kierkegaard, and Fyodor Dostoevsky were all a significant help, but I needed something that spoke more directly to the time in which I was living. I needed a deep well dug in my own time and place. What did Jesus say about seeking and finding? My seeking heart was about to be rewarded.

On a summer afternoon I was at home browsing my bookshelves. I was deliberately looking for a book that would "give me a breakthrough." I couldn't settle on anything. So I prayed, "God, show me what to read." And I sensed...nothing. I went downstairs feeling a bit agitated and slumped into a chair. Within a minute or two my wife, Peri, walked into the room, handed me a book and said, "I think you should read this." She knew nothing of my moments ago prayer, but she had just handed me a book, and told me to read it. This was my Augustine-like "take and read" moment. It sent chills down my spine. Somehow I knew it was the answer to my prayer. The book was Dallas Willard's *The Divine Conspiracy*. The strange thing was Peri had not read this book and had no more idea who Dallas Willard was than I did. (As I said, I was embarrassingly ignorant of the good stuff.) Neither of us were sure how the book had even made its way into our house. But, oh my, was it ever an answer to prayer! The next day I was flying somewhere and I took out the book providentially given to me by an angel. I began to read. And my life changed forever. Hyperbole? No. Stone cold fact. Reading Dallas Willard's *The Divine Conspiracy* was like having a door kicked open in my mind. It opened my eyes to the kingdom of God. And the kingdom of God is, well, everything! In his foreword to *The Divine Conspiracy*, Richard Foster writes:

> *The Divine Conspiracy* is the book I have been searching for all my life. Like Michelangelo's Sistine ceiling, it is a masterpiece and a wonder... I would place *The Divine Conspiracy* in rare company indeed: along-side the writings of Dietrich Bonhoeffer and John Wesley, John Calvin and Martin Luther, Teresa of Avila and Hildegard of Bingen, and perhaps even Thomas Aquinas and Augustine of Hippo. If the *parousia* tarries, this is a book for the next millennium.[5]

That's exactly what I needed! Augustine and Aquinas for the twenty-first century! Dallas Willard was my gateway to the good stuff. Directly or indirectly reading Willard led me to others: N.T. Wright, Walter Brueggemann, Eugene Peterson, Frederick Buechner, Stanley Hauerwas, John Howard Yoder, René Girard, Miroslav Volf, Karl Barth, Hans Urs von Balthasar, David Bentley Hart, Wendell Berry, Scot McKnight, Thomas Merton, Richard Rohr, and so many more. I couldn't read fast enough. Night after night I was up past midnight reading, reading, reading. I was making up for lost time. I kept thinking, "Where have you been all my life?!" I had struck gold and I couldn't pull it out of the ground fast enough. I was now a gold miner.

I became a self-imposed prisoner in my own late night seminary. Over the next couple of years I read myself into a completely new and much richer place. How did it begin? With a crazy twenty-two day fast and a whispered prayer—"God, show me what to read."

When I reflect upon the seminal year of 2004, I think of it as a strange mixture of pain and discovery. I was thrilled with what I was finding, but not everyone in my church shared my enthusiasm. The gold I was discovering was changing my preaching—significantly. But not everyone liked the change. People I had known, loved, and led for many years were beginning to dig their heels in or bail out. Some didn't like my "new direction." They couldn't see what I saw with what I called my "new eyes." In their frustration they lashed out. Some said I was becoming "emergent." (I honestly didn't even know what that was—and I don't think they did either.) Others said I was becoming "liberal" or "too intellectual." Some of my less articulate critics simply opted for "backslidden." One Sunday morning a longtime church member cornered me with a harangue about what had happened to "the real Pastor Brian." According to his assessment I had ceased to be myself and had become an imposter. These comments hurt. People leaving hurt. It hurt more than I let on. But there was no going back. I couldn't un-know what I knew and be true to myself. The pain of being misunderstood and misrepresented was part of the price for obtaining the vintage wine of substantive Christianity. No matter what others thought, I knew what was happening. I was saving my soul. I was discovering Jesus afresh. I was encountering an unvarnished

Jesus, a Jesus free from the lacquer of cheap religious certitude, tawdry motivational jargon, and partisan political agenda. I was being born again…again. I was gaining new eyes. I was seeing the kingdom of God, really for the first time. I was transitioning from water to wine, from grape soda to Brunello di Montalcino.

During our years of transition there were times when the pressure was almost unbearable. It's one thing to make a major theological course correction in midlife, it's another thing to do so publically while leading a large church and trying to hold it all together. I mean, I'm pretty sure I'm the only pastor to have hosted both Jesse Duplantis and Walter Brueggemann as guest speakers. That may give you some idea of what I mean by "transition." We had journeyed from hosting prosperity gospel televangelists to conducting conferences with respected theologians. But trying to hold everything together during such a radical transition created a lot of pressure.

Those were days of pressure and pain. The pressure came from living on

> My specialty had been the idol of certitude. An ever-popular idol. I knew how to give easy answers, claim the promises, and cast everything in black and white.

the fault line between two shifting tectonic plates. One plate was moving me away from a compromised Christianity co-opted by consumerism. The other plate moved stubbornly in the direction of the pragmatic need to maintain a viable congregation. I wanted to be faithful to lead my church in a new and better direction, but I didn't want to go about it in a reckless manner. Inevitably I would feel guilty about whatever decision I made. I would feel guilty about making changes too slowly and I would feel guilty about making changes too quickly…at the same time! It was the pressure of what felt like an impossible situation. The pain came from being misunderstood, vilified, and rejected by people I had considered friends. Rarely did these people actually talk with me. More often they would just leave the church, send a hateful email, and begin a campaign to persuade others that I was more or less apostate. Some of these were people to whom I had been a good friend and faithful pastor. I had baptized them, baptized their children, counseled them, encouraged them, taught them, supported them, prayed for and with them. To have them leave without a face-to-face, heart-to-heart conversation and act like an enemy was the infliction of a painful wound.

When the pressure would become too great, Peri and I would try to sneak away for a few days to our beloved Rocky Mountain National Park. It was healing for our souls to hike in the mountains, be in the quiet wilderness, and have long talks about Jesus and how wonderful it is to be on the journey of discovery together, even if there was pain involved. It was therapy of the best kind. On one of our mountain escapes I was reading Eugene Peterson's dazzling *Christ Plays In Ten Thousand Places*. During a bumpy flight home from Denver to Kansas City I read this passage:

> A huge religious marketplace has been set up in North America to meet the needs and fantasies of people just like us. There are conferences and gatherings custom-designed to give us what we need. Books and videos and seminars promise to let us in on the Christian "secret" of whatever we feel is lacking in our life: financial security, well-behaved children, weight-loss, exotic sex, travel to

holy sites, exciting worship, celebrity teachers. The people who promote these goods and services all smile a lot and are good-looking… We have become consumers of packaged spiritualities. This is idolatry. We never think of using this term for it since everything we are buying or paying for is defined by the adjective "Christian." But idolatry it is nevertheless: God packaged as a product; God depersonalized and made available as a technique or program. The Christian market in idols has never been more brisk or lucrative.[6]

Reading those words seven miles above the Midwestern plains somewhere between Denver and Kansas City, I recognized my former self in that paragraph. I had been both a purchaser and purveyor of Christian idols (yet always with sincere intentions). My specialty had been the idol of certitude. An ever-popular idol. I knew how to give easy answers, claim the promises, and cast everything in black and white. I was sure of everything. But all of that had changed. Among the things that died during my twenty-two day "death vigil" was certitude. Arrogant certitude was giving way to the ambiguity of authentic faith. I stopped reading at Peterson's paragraph on Christian idols—"God packaged as product"—and as our plane shuddered in the turbulence, I scribbled these words in the back of *Christ Plays In Ten Thousand Places*:

Turbulance

I was once so sure
So sure of myself

So sure that what I wanted
Was one in the same with what God wanted
How could it be otherwise?
Child of God that I am

I was once so sure
I was taught to assert my will
In the name of the Lord, to be sure
For the name of the Lord is a talisman
To endorse and empower my will to be done
For what else could my god have to do
But to make all my wishes and dreams come true?

I was once so sure
That I knew what was good for me
And what was good for me
Was good things for me
Me. Me. Me. Me. Me. Me. Me.
Oh, I knew better than to say it just so
I knew how to dress it up in altruistic robes
And how to crown it with chapter and verse
Nothing like a plucked verse to make you so sure
(Yet it and I weren't all bad, oh no, far from it)

But the point of this confession is
I was once so sure
That I knew good and evil, right and wrong
In me, in thee, in theology, in policy
But there's a snake that lives in that tree

Is original sin a sin of epistemology?
To be so sure
Certitude in doctrine and politics
And just where the dividing line runs
Safe in the certain knowledge
That I'm on the right side
Of the right-and-wrong line
I was once so sure
And it's fun being so sure
People like it when you're so sure
(If they share your certainty)
And isn't that what faith is?
Being so sure?
Well…
I'm not so sure
Cock-sure, can't-miss certainty
Is not the faith that I see
When I look at the patriarchs, prophets, and poets
And Jesus
("My God, My God, why have you forsaken me?")
At the cross faith and hope find their finest hour
But arrogant certitude is proved to be an impostor
(Did I hear the cock crow?)

Instead of brashness and bravado
The poet of hope said
"In quietness and trust"
So now when I'm not so sure
I try to be quiet and trust

Not myself, my mind, my kind
But in the mercy of God
In his severe salvation
A salvation that is sweet as honey
And severe as the cross
Though he slay me
Yet will I trust him
Surely
Goodness and Mercy

Later, when I shared my composed-in-the-clouds autobiographical poem (or whatever it was), I was surprised by how many people were upset by it. In retrospect I was too naïve and should not have been surprised. I had hoped everyone would share my enthusiasm for embracing a more honest faith, but this was not the case. Some misunderstood my honesty as a tacit compromise with unbelief. That's not what it is. It's a repudiation of certitude masquerading as faith. Certitude is a poor substitute for authentic faith. But certitude is popular; it's popular because it's easy. If all you want is cheap certitude, just land on some opinion one way or the other, tell yourself you're certain, and that's that. No wrestling with doubt, no dark night of the soul, no costly agonizing over the matter, no testing yourself with hard questions. Just accept a secondhand assumption or a majority opinion or a popular sentiment as the final word and settle into certainty. You don't have to think about it ever again. Ignorance is bliss, but so is

> Ignorance is bliss, but so is certitude—they're first cousins. Yet none of this is to be confused with faith.

certitude—they're first cousins. Yet none of this is to be confused with faith. George MacDonald, the Scottish writer whose works had such a profound influence on C.S. Lewis, said this:

> Do you love your faith so little that you have never battled a single fear lest your faith should not be true? Where there are no doubts, no questions, no perplexities, there can be no growth.[7]

George MacDonald wrote that in his novel *The Curate's Awakening*. Now I was an awakening curate—or pastor, anyway. I was awakening to the cost of real faith. Real faith will cost you. Real faith is forged in the fiery theodicy of Job's bitter trial where every assumption of the goodness of God is put to the test. Real faith is found during the forty-day wilderness temptation where the first question from the tempter is, "Are you sure?" Real faith reaches the apex of "Father, into your hands I commit my spirit" only after the agonizing cry of "My God, my God, why have you forsaken me?" We have to wrestle with doubt to arrive at real faith. Certitude can't be bothered with all that. Real faith has room for doubt—understanding that the effort to believe is the very thing that makes doubt possible. Real faith is not afraid of doubt, but the faux faith of certitude is afraid of its own shadow. I have no idea how to arrive at real faith without a journey involving doubt. The mistake of pop apologetics—the silly kind that looks for an ancient boat on a Turkish mountaintop or Egyptian chariots on the bottom of the Red Sea—is that it is an attempt to do away with the need for faith altogether! The Noah's Ark hunters want to "prove" God so that faith will be unnecessary. But God does not traffic in the empirically verifiable. God refuses to prove himself and perform circus tricks at our behest in order to obliterate doubt. Frederick Buechner says it this way:

> Without somehow destroying me in the process, how could God reveal himself in a way that would leave no room for doubt? If there were no room for doubt, there would be no room for me.[8]

In the days of my certitude there was no room for me. I learned how to parrot the party line. To say what was expected. What was expected was a mixture of fundamentalist biblicism, word of faith success, and religious right triumphalism. None of that was me. The real me had always been more complex than that. But in the world of religious certitude there is no room to think, no room for nuance and complexity, no room to nurture the soul of a mystic. In my search for success in the world of Americanized Christianity, the real me was being erased. After the transformative year of 2004 I wanted to become myself again…while there was still time. I had already lost too much time, I didn't want to lose my soul to an enforced conformity. These thoughts occupied my mind with a sense of impending crisis. I felt an urgency that something had to be done, but what?

Jason Upton, a Christian recording artist and a good friend, was ministering in our church. Following the concert, Jason and his band were hanging out in my study. There were several conversations going on, mostly about music. At some point during the evening Jason wrote these two words on a note pad he found on my desk, "Kierkegaard. Provocations." I discovered the note the next morning. I wasn't sure what it meant. A few days later I was in a bookstore and saw *Provocations* by Søren Kierkegaard on the shelf among the new releases. It was a new collection of Kierkegaard's spiritual writings that had just been published. I started reading it right there in the bookstore. The first chapter in *Provocations* is entitled "Dare to Decide" and it opens with these words:

> Can there be something in life that has power over us which little by little causes us to forget all that is good? And can this ever happen to anyone who has heard the call of eternity quite clearly and strongly? If this can ever be, then one must look for a cure against it. Praise be to God that such a cure exists—to quietly make a decision. A decision joins us to the eternal. It brings what is eternal into time. A decision raises us with a shock from the slumber of monotony. A decision breaks the long row of weary thoughts. A decision pronounces its blessing upon even the weakest beginning, as long as it is a real beginning. Decision is the awakening to the eternal.[9]

A long time ago I had heard what Kierkegaard describes as "the call of eternity" and I had heard it "quite clearly and strongly." When I was fifteen years old I launched into the thrilling adventure of following Jesus. But thirty years had gone by. Was I now doomed to succumb to the slumber of monotony in midlife? I didn't want that. But I also knew that to move away from the kind of Christianity that had given me "success" was a daring thing to do. It would entail risk. To be true to the call of Christ and to save my true self I had to be willing to sacrifice success and risk failure. Would I dare?

A few weeks later I was walking through the Detroit airport on one of those moving walkways thinking about these things when I suddenly crossed a threshold in my mind. I made a decision. A daring decision. A risky decision. I had reached the point of no return—there would be no going back. I wanted to be my true self. Suddenly I said out loud, "Now with the help of God I shall become myself!" The curious glances I drew from strangers in the Detroit airport bothered me not in the least. I had made a decision. I was on the road to recovery. I was recovering my soul. Water was turning to wine.

Chapter 2

Five Words

After the first twenty-two days of 2004 and the discoveries that followed I felt like I had been shot from a cannon and landed in a new world. This was more than a little disorienting, not only for me, but for our church as well. It was clear that we were heading in a new direction, but what was it? We had embarked upon a journey, but where were we going? I needed language to communicate what was happening. I needed signposts to help find my way in a new frontier. Something big had happened, but I needed help with communication and navigation. It was late August and our leadership team was going on a three-day retreat. I needed to speak clearly about what I was sensing, about the new direction for Word of Life. Three days before the retreat I prayed a simple prayer, "Jesus, tell me what to say." As soon as I prayed that prayer, five words shot into my mind. They came as quickly as I could write them down. I didn't conjure them from within; they came as words from elsewhere.

Cross

Mystery

Eclectic

Community

Revolution

Just like that. Just that quick. I didn't "think" these five words, I just wrote them down. Cross, mystery, eclectic, community, revolution. At the time I had no idea that those five words hastily scribbled in a Moleskin notebook would help guide and define our church for the next decade. Over the next few days I shared the Five Words with our leadership team, trying to expand them as best I could. Later I preached them repeatedly to our church. I spoke on the Five Words frequently in pastors' conferences. Over time I came to understand what the Five Words really were; they were a way to reorient myself within the Christian faith. They were signposts to navigate a theological transition. Most of all they were five fresh words to replace five tired "isms"—"isms" that were sucking the life out of the Christianity I knew, "isms" I had to replace.

Consumerism

Fundamentalism

Sectarianism

Individualism

Politicism

These five "isms" had characterized and distorted the Christianity I had known, and it was time for a major overhaul. The Five Words were true signposts to guide me into a deeper, richer, fuller Christianity.

CROSS

Other than a wedding ring, I've never been much for jewelry. No rings, no necklaces, no bracelets. It's just not my style. But after I embarked upon my great transition I bought a necklace. To be more precise I bought a small bronze cross that I attached to a leather cord. It was a fifth-century Byzantine cross purchased from an antiquities dealer in the Old City of Jerusalem. I wanted this little relic because with my new eyes I was seeing the cross in a new way. The crosses that proliferate around the Church of the Holy Sepulchre seemed to beckon to me. In the ancient ruins of Beit She'an in Northern Israel I saw a Byzantine cross painted over a baptistery in a fifth-century church situated near a pagan temple. It moved me in a strange way. I tried to imagine people being baptized under that painted cross. The power of the cross as the universally recognized symbol of the Christian faith had captured my imagination in a way it never had before. I longed for a tangible connection to the roots of my Christian faith. That's why I bought the ancient cross. From time to time I wonder about its original owner. Was he a priest connected to the Church of the Holy Sepulchre? Was she a pilgrim from Constantinople? I'll never know, but we are connected by a common cross and a shared faith. I rarely wear the cross. It hangs from a lamp over my desk in my study. I see it every time I write a sermon. Later I bought a Russian

cross icon in Bethlehem. It sits on my writing desk. It watches over
every book I've written. This seems important to me. I want my
work to be done in the light of the cross.

If the purpose of the Five Words was to reorient myself and
our church within the Christian faith, then the first of the Five
Words *had* to be "Cross." Of course it did. The cross is the
indisputable epicenter of Christian faith. But what does it mean?
After two millennia of Christianity, it's easy for the cross to fade
into a feeble cliché, to be ignored as a sentimental but largely
meaningless symbol. Perhaps this was the reason I had never really
embraced the symbol of the cross. But now things were changing
and for the first time I was struck by the fact that there was no
cross in our worship space. The cross as a symbol seemed too
archaic to have contemporary relevance in our charismatic church.
We just never felt the need to have one. But after August 2004 I
knew I needed to think about the cross in a fresh and deeper way.
So I began to contemplate the cross during extended periods of
prayer. I would read a gospel portion on the crucifixion and then
try to transport myself to Calvary. I attempted to join John the
Beloved and the Galilean women and the Roman centurion as a
silent witness to the death of Jesus. I started to incorporate an
Orthodox crucifixion icon to help focus my contemplation. Over
time I began to see the cross in a much deeper way—not as a mere
factor in an atonement theory equation, but as the moment in
time and space where God reclaimed creation. I saw the cross as
the place where Jesus refounded the world. Instead of being
organized around an axis of power enforced by violence, at the
cross the world was refounded around an axis of love expressed in
forgiveness. Imagine this pivotal moment in history—Jesus

crucified, hanging on a tree, arms outstretched in proffered embrace, showing the world the heart of God, and praying, "Father, forgive them, for they know not what they do." Christianity looks like that—Christianity looks like love absorbing sin and death, trusting God for resurrection.

Seen in the light of the Easter dawn, the cross is revealed to be the lost Tree of Life. In the middle of a world dominated by death, the Tree of Life is rediscovered in the form of a Roman cross. The cross is the act of radical forgiveness that gives sin, violence, and retribution a place to die in the body of Jesus. The world that was born when Adam and Eve in their shame began to blame, the world where violent Cain killed innocent Abel, the world of pride and power that tramples the meek and weak—at the cross *that* world sinned its sins into Jesus Christ. And what happens? Jesus forgives. Why? Because God is like that. In the defining moment of the cross Jesus defines what God is really like. God is love—co-suffering, all-forgiving, sin-absorbing, never-ending love. God is not like Caiaphas sacrificing a scapegoat. God is not like Pilate enacting justice by violence. God is like Jesus, absorbing and forgiving sin.

> God is not like Caiaphas sacrificing a scapegoat. God is not like Pilate enacting justice by violence. God is like Jesus, absorbing and forgiving sin.

At the cross a world of sin is absorbed by the love of God and recycled into grace and mercy. *This* is what the cross is about! This is what Christianity reveals. Christianity is not about success-in-life sermons where we learn to be "winners" in the competitive game of life. Life is not a game, life is a gift. Life is not about competition, life is about love. Life is not about winning the game, getting to the top, coming in first—that's the old world of Cain and Pharaoh and Caesar. The world of cold-blooded competition is the world that kills Christ. In his defining moment Jesus shames the way of Cain, Pharaoh, and Caesar. At the cross Jesus reveals that life is about learning to love, even if you have to die to do it, because you know that beyond death is the love of the Father and resurrection of the dead. This is the cross. This is Christianity.

This was not the Christianity I had known in its word-of-faith, religious-right, success-in-life aberrations. Meditation on the cross pointed me to something deeper, richer, fuller, and infinitely more costly. Deep contemplation on the cross became a form of shock therapy—a radical reorientation that revealed how disturbingly distorted much of Americanized Christianity has become. The cross of Christ poses a serious challenge to the popular consumer Christianity dominant in North America—easy-cheesy-cotton-candy-Christianity. After 2004, I was through being a hawker of a cotton candy gospel offered at the three-ring circus of an entertainment-oriented Christianity. No more sickly sweet spun sugar. Now it would be flesh and blood! In the bread and wine of the Eucharist Jesus calls us to eat his flesh and drink his blood—cotton candy doesn't belong on the altar. But our spiritual "sugar addiction" is not easy to break.

As Americans we are given a script from birth—it is our shared and assumed formula for the pursuit of happiness. Without even being aware of it we are scripted in the belief that our superior technology, our self-help ideology, our dominant military, and our capacity to obtain consumer goods should guarantee our happiness—our ticket to Paradise. Said just so, it sounds silly, but when it is communicated in the liturgies of advertising and the propaganda of state, it becomes believable…and we do believe it. *Give me a new iPhone, a motivational talk, a trillion-dollar war machine, a Visa card, and I can be happy!* For the most part the Americanized church has unconsciously bought into this script and concocted a compromised Christianity to endorse the script point for point. It's Americanism with a Jesus fish bumper sticker. But in the end the desperate pursuit of the brass ring of happiness—even when "Christianized" by the prosperity gospel—leads to a shriveled and disappointed soul. And worse, it leads to a misspent life. In the final analysis the American script is shamed by the cross of Christ.

The Enlightenment promise that technology would lead to Utopia has been weighed in the balances of history and found wanting. It went up in smoke—*literal smoke!*—in the gray ashes of Auschwitz and a hideous mushroom cloud over Hiroshima. Gullible faith in the ability of technology to automatically produce a better world should now be seen as a naïve anachronism.

A Christian obsession with therapeutic self-help fads reveals how disconnected we are from substantive historic theology and the ancient practice of spiritual direction. Today we have pastors mimicking one another by replacing their pulpit with a bed and giving their congregation a "thirty-day sex challenge." Please. These silly gimmicks oscillate between ludicrous and pathetic.

Superstitious reverence for all things military constantly verges on the idolatrous and prevents the church from being a prophetic people. Memorial Day is not on the church calendar, and military color guards marching down church aisles with rifles on their shoulders should not be part of our liturgy.

Consumerism, as much as anything, has come to define much of America's most visible expressions of Christianity. Take a quick stroll though "Christian TV Land" and you'll see what I mean. This is what Janis Joplin mocked when she sang, "Oh Lord, won't you buy me a Mercedes Benz." The cross heaps shame on all of this.

The American prescription for happiness is the script we've been handed. But it's a lie. It's a false gospel, yet enormously popular. The only possible way to resist that dominant script is through the adoption of what Walter Brueggemann calls a counterscript. For the Christian that counterscript is the gospel of Jesus Christ—at the center of which stands a cross! When we are trying to relocate the center of authentic Christianity the first word is always "cross." Jesus promised paradise, not to those who prioritize personal happiness, but to one who was dying on a cross beside him. Father John Behr closes his brilliant little book *Becoming Human* with this meditation on the cross:

> Our journey through this world, dying to this world as "Egypt," through baptism, then dying as we sojourn in the desert of this world by taking up the cross daily, refashions us as living human beings, human beings living in this world as God's paradise at the center of which stand the cross, the tree of life. "Truly I say to you, today you will be with me in Paradise," says Christ to the one willing to be crucified with him. Are we ready, now, to live?[1]

In contemplating the cross I found the portal to the deeper, richer, fuller Christianity I had been secretly longing for. But the cross is a costly portal. The price of admission is death. It means losing your false life to find your true life. The path to paradise is often the path of suffering. If our chief goal is to avoid suffering, we will probably never find paradise. Paradise is not found in the mall, it's found on the Easter side of Good Friday.

MYSTERY

The first time Peri and I were in Jerusalem was in 1996. After landing in Tel Aviv and driving to Jerusalem we checked into our hotel quite late. We were tired from the long travel, but I just had to explore this most alluring of cities—the city of the Hebrew kings and prophets, the city of Jesus and the Apostles. I couldn't wait until morning. So under the light of a full moon on a quiet Shabbat night, we walked a few blocks to the Jaffa Gate, past the ancient walls built by Suleiman the Magnificent and entered a mysterious world of ghostly shadows, cobblestone streets, and sacred stories. We didn't know where we were going. The shops were closed. Very few people were around. We wandered the labyrinth of narrow streets and got lost. But we didn't care. We were exploring a mystery—a mystery that was deeply connected to our faith. The fatigue of transcontinental travel was overcome by the energy of entering a mystery. I've never forgotten that night. It's a favorite memory. It was the overwhelming sense of mystery that made that night so magical and memorable. Years later I would discover that my faith needed more mystery if I was going to maintain energy over the long haul.

Mystery is the word that replaces the "ism" known as fundamentalism. Fundamentalism was born as the wrongheaded reaction to the crisis of modernity. Ironically, fundamentalism is an approach to faith that accepts modernity's now discredited claim that empiricism is the sole source of knowledge. Feeling intimidated by the Scientific Revolution, fundamentalism takes a "scientific" approach to the Bible—which is perhaps the worst of all ways to approach Scripture. The Bible is not interested in giving (or even competing with) scientific explanations. The Bible is working on a different project than scientific inquiry. What Scripture gives us is inspired glimpses into the divine mystery. The point is never to "prove" the Bible, but to enter into the mystery through the portal of Scripture. The Bible has no interest in "proving" itself—it has no need to do this and makes no attempt to do so. The Bible is not a scientific text or even an end in itself, the Bible is the Spirit-inspired sign that points us to the true Word of God—the Word made flesh, the greatest of all sacred mysteries. Any approach to the Incarnation that does not treat it as a sacred mystery is an act of desecration. If we insist on explaining the mysteries of faith—mysteries like the Trinity, the Incarnation, the Resurrection, the Ascension, the return of Christ, the new birth, baptism, the Eucharist—we inevitably reduce rich mysteries to cheap certitudes. This is the bane of fundamentalism. In the search for certitude and a penchant for Bible-Answer-Man explanations, the intrinsically artistic nature of the Christian mystery is turned into gift shop trinkets. Fundamentalism is to Christianity what paint-by-numbers is to art.

With the second of the Five Words I was able to identify an ache that had always been in my soul—it was the ache for mystery. Mystery is at the heart of reality. But don't take my word for it, ask a quantum physicist! Cutting edge theoretical physics has discovered it has plenty of use for the word mystery. Newtonian physics sought to explain everything, but post-Einstein physics has learned to bow in chastened reverence before the altar of mystery. And a Christian should have at least as much reverence for the mystery of being as a quantum physicist!

Christianity is a sacred mystery. The Apostle Paul loves to speak of mystery—he uses that rich word twenty-one times in his letters. Christianity is a *confession,* not an *explanation.* We will attempt to explain what we legitimately can, but we will always confess more than we can explain. I fully confess God is Father, Son, and Holy Spirit, even though I cannot fully explain the Trinity. I fully confess the resurrection of Jesus Christ, even though I cannot fully explain what it means that the Son of God has inaugurated a world beyond the realm of death. I fully confess that Christ will come again, even though I think those "end time prophecy charts" are utterly ridiculous. (And wrong!) Room for mystery is necessary for orthodox theology. Mystery is good for theology. And mystery is good for the soul.

> Christianity is a *confession,* not an *explanation.* We will attempt to explain what we legitimately can, but we will always confess more than we can explain.

Freed from the shackles of certitude, the postmodern soul not only accepts the presence of mystery, it craves it. In the nineteenth century what passed for mystery was a Sherlock Holmes adventure—which is to say, there was no mystery at all, just a problem to be solved. *Elementary, my dear Watson.* When I was a kid there were those lousy Scooby-Doo mystery cartoons. Again, no mystery...just a guy in a mask...every time. But that is not reality, scientific or otherwise. Ask Nils Bohr about God playing dice or Werner Heisenberg about the impossibility of certainty or Erwin Schrödinger about his cat, and these imminent physicists will tell you the universe is *full* of mystery.

During my lifetime mystery has made a comeback in pop culture. We've gone from Sherlock Holmes and Scooby-Doo to *The X-Files* and *LOST*…and discovered that mystery is good for the soul. What I'm trying to say is that *The X-Files* is better than Scooby-Doo! Mystery is *not* a problem to be solved—mystery is an integral aspect of being to be honored. If we want to eliminate all mystery we will do bad science, as quantum physics now suggests. The same can be said of theology. If we want to eliminate all mystery we will do bad theology and produce an inferior Christianity. A Christianity that embraces sacred mystery is the way beyond an Enlightenment-bound Christianity genuflecting at the altar of empiricism.

Taking its cues from the scientism of a bygone era, Western Christianity has tried for too long to make the gospel a kind of scientific formula—a pseudo-science of biblical facts, atonement theories, and sinners' prayers—when it's more like a song, a symphony, a poem, a painting, a drama, a dance, and, yes, a mystery. The Industrial Revolution of the nineteenth century saw the artisan replaced with conveyer-belted, smoke-belching factories. Things would no longer be handcrafted, they would now be mass-produced. Christianity followed suit. The revivalism of the nineteenth and twentieth centuries sought to "industrialize" evangelism. While Henry Ford was mass-producing cars, Billy Sunday was mass-producing converts. Except it doesn't work that way. Listen to what Jesus says to Nicodemus about being born of the Spirit:

> So don't be surprised when I say, "You must be born again." The wind blows where it wants. Just as you can hear the wind but can't tell where it comes from or where it is going, *so you can't explain how people are born of the Spirit.* (John 3:7–8, New Living Translation, emphasis added)

Jesus says we can't explain how people are born of the Spirit. The irony is, we've done just the opposite—we've *completely* explained how people are born again! We know the five points, the four laws, and the three steps. There is no mystery. *Here, accept this atonement theory, pray this manufactured prayer, and—presto!—you're born again.* No mystery to it. Just a cheap, formulaic, mass-produced, one-size-fits-all conversion. No wonder the vast majority of these "conversions" turn out to be defective. The Spirit of God is an artisan, not an industrialist. Meditation on the sacred mysteries revealed and confessed in the Christian faith is the alternative for the know-it-all fundamentalism that is about as satisfying to the soul as a Scooby-Doo cartoon. The Spirit blows where it wants, and you can't tell where it comes from or where it is going. All hail the Sacred Mystery!

ECLECTIC

Over the years I've received a lot of speaking invitations, but I'll never forget when I was invited to speak to the Benedictine Sisters of Perpetual Adoration in Clyde, Missouri. The sisters had read one of my books and were inviting me to speak to them at their monastery. I gladly accepted. Then they asked, "What is your fee?" I've never had a speaking fee, so I just replied, "What's my fee? A meal and a conversation." They said they could gladly do that. When I arrived at the monastery I kept smelling toast. It turns out the sisters in Clyde bake the Communion wafers for most of the Catholic churches in America. It's one of the ways they support themselves.

So there I was at a Catholic monastery founded by Swiss nuns in 1874 that smelled like toast. I really don't get nervous before speaking, but standing in front of forty Catholic nuns in a monastery was unfamiliar ground for me. I wasn't sure what the proper decorum was for a Protestant pastor in a Catholic monastery, so I just decided to be myself and spoke on the topic of Christian forgiveness. After I concluded my talk and sat down, the prioress asked if I would speak some more. I thought she meant would I come back and speak on another occasion and I indicated I would be happy to return. But the prioress said, "I mean would you speak some more right now?" That was a surprise. I've spoken in hundreds of "on fire for Jesus" churches over the years, but the first and only time I've been called back to the stage for an encore was in a Catholic monastery! I wouldn't have predicted that. Since then Peri and I have become quite close to the sisters in Clyde. I consider them dear friends. But there had been a time in my life when a deep spiritual friendship with Catholic nuns would have been inconceivable.

> By restricting my Christianity to the narrow confines of modern charismatic evangelicalism, I suffered from a self-inflicted theological poverty.

Prior to 2004 I was a poverty-stricken Christian...and I didn't even know it. My poverty was theological and it was the sad consequence of my arrogant sectarianism. By restricting my Christianity to the narrow confines of modern charismatic evangelicalism, I suffered from a self-inflicted theological poverty. I needed the riches of the whole church. I needed to be able to draw upon the broad spectrum of Christian thinkers and theologians, mystics and writers. I needed to become eclectic in my approach to Christianity. A Christianity that is sufficiently broad and eclectic liberates us from an arrogant and impoverished sectarianism.

In my youthful arrogance (the word I really want to use is stupidity) I effectively defined and limited Christianity to *my kind* of Christianity —a charismatic-flavored evangelicalism. As far as I was concerned, most Catholics, Orthodox, Anglicans, and mainline Protestants needed to "get saved"—which is to say, they needed to become my style of Christian. There were times in my twenties and thirties when I was particularly antagonistic toward Catholics and mainline Protestants. I thought Catholics belonged to the "whore of Babylon" and mainliners were all "liberal goats." How egotistical! How stupid! I'm ashamed of all that now. I have repented. Which means I've called my former attitude sinful and changed my mind—I simply don't think that way anymore.

Today my theological reading is pretty evenly divided between Orthodox, Catholic, Anglican, Protestant, and Evangelical writers. I want to help all kinds of people discover a vibrant personal faith in the living Christ, but I feel no need to convert my Orthodox and Catholic brothers and sisters to a Protestant version of Christianity. From my vantage point I've come to think that Orthodox, Catholic, Anglican, Protestant, and Evangelical expressions of Christianity generally have the same amount of truth—it just depends on what areas of truth you want to focus on. Yes, I actually believe this! I honestly don't think evangelicalism has a greater claim to Christian truth than Catholicism. It's true that I'm not entirely comfortable with the Catholic view of Mary and the practice of a male-only celibate priesthood. But neither am I comfortable with the Protestant view of *Sola Scriptura* and the emphasis on radical individualism. Another way of saying it might be like this—we need the whole body of Christ to properly form the body of Christ. This much I'm sure of, Orthodox mystery, Catholic beauty, Anglican liturgy, Protestant audacity, Evangelical energy, Charismatic reality—I need it all!

Over the past decade I've learned to worship with my Orthodox, Catholic, Anglican, and mainline brothers and sisters; I've found it beautiful and deeply rewarding. If my circumstances were different, I could imagine myself belonging to any one of these branches of Christianity. As it is, I'm content with being an eclectic Christian…or perhaps an eclectic sacramental evangelical. I've found that within the wide orthodoxy defined by the historic Christian creeds there is room for a lot of different expressions of our shared faith. As I glance around my writing table I see twelve books on Saint Francis of Assisi, an Orthodox icon, an Anglican prayer book, and a volume of Karl Barth's *Dogmatics*. I have no intention of surrendering any of these to the petulant sectarians who want to police such things. As Thomas Merton stated:

> If I can unite in myself the thought and the devotion of Eastern and Western Christendom, the Greek and the Latin Fathers, the Russian with the Spanish mystics, I can prepare in myself the reunion of divided Christians. … If we want to

bring together what is divided, we cannot do so by imposing one division upon the other. If we do this, the union is not Christian. It is political and doomed to further conflict. We must contain all the divided worlds in ourselves and transcend them in Christ.[2]

When I was converted from sectarian to eclectic, I obtained a passport that allowed me to travel freely throughout the whole body of Christ. In my theological travels I have discovered a Christianity that has both historical depth and ecumenical width. Now I can't imagine not being able to access all the great contributors to contemporary Christian thought. Orthodox thinkers like Kallistos Ware and David Bentley Hart. Catholic thinkers like Richard Rohr and William Cavanaugh. Anglican thinkers like Rowen Williams and N.T. Wright. Mainline thinkers like Walter Brueggemann and Eugene Peterson. Without them my Christianity would be horribly impoverished.

> When I was converted from sectarian to eclectic, I obtained a passport that allowed me to travel freely throughout the whole body of Christ. In my theological travels I have discovered a Christianity that has both historical depth and ecumenical width.

After my book *Unconditional?* was published in 2010—a book on the centrality of forgiveness in the Christian faith—I began to receive a much wider range of speaking invitations. I spoke at the monastery of Benedictine nuns. I spoke to a group of progressive mainline pastors. I spoke at one of the largest Lutheran churches in

America. I participated in a panel discussion with Catholic intellectuals in Lisbon. But not only did I speak in these different settings, I made friends among them. I was discovering how much I really like the whole body of Christ! I have no interest in trying to convert my friends from one expression of Christianity to another. Do I think the Benedictine nuns should become Protestants? Do I think the Orthodox priests I've come to know and love should become Pentecostals? Do I think my pastor friends among the progressive mainline Protestants should become conservative evangelicals? Of course not! We need Benedictine nuns. We need Orthodox priests. We need mainline ministers. And we may even need a few eclectic sacramental evangelical pastors…or whatever it is I am.

COMMUNITY

My initial encounter with Jesus Christ occurred during the height of the Jesus Movement. This was a kind of spiritual version of the counterculture movement which swept across the United States and other parts of the world in the early seventies, bringing millions of young people to faith in Christ. The Jesus Movement was the matrix of the Vineyard and Calvary Chapel movements, introducing contemporary worship music to the wider church.

Almost immediately I became involved in a Christian coffeehouse in St. Joseph called the Catacombs. It was basically a small venue for Christian concerts and occasional teaching. We first met in a basement below a dive bar, then in a Salvation Army quonset hut, and finally in a storefront next to a biker bar on St. Joseph Avenue. Jesus music artists like Keith Green, Second

Chapter of Acts, Sweet Comfort Band, and Paul Clark performed at the Catacombs. At the age of seventeen I was leading the Catacombs, which would eventually turn into Word of Life Church. But the thing I remember most about the Catacombs wasn't the music or ministry, but the intense experience of community. We were young people in our teens and twenties doing life together, hanging out together nearly every night of the week. We had a deep sense that we belonged, not only to Jesus, but to one another. To this day when I read the Book of Acts it reminds me of the kind of community those of us connected to the Catacombs experienced. Yet it seems we couldn't hold on to that forever. Eventually we faded into the dominant American experience of individualism overshadowing community. Being a Christian became mostly something we do alone.

One of the biggest changes that came about after my 2004 seismic shift was in my basic understanding of the nature of salvation. As an evangelical Protestant I had inherited a highly individualistic approach to salvation. I, along with nearly everyone I knew, viewed salvation as primarily a private transaction between God and the solitary individual. Jesus was handing out tickets to a gated community in heaven where everyone would have their own private mansion. The church's role was reduced to that of a superfluous common interest club. The church was seen as peripheral, not integral to salvation. It's like a cyclist who joins a cycling club to enhance the individual experience of cycling. But if the cyclist decides she doesn't like her fellow club members, or doesn't want to go on the Sunday morning group rides, or no longer wants to pay her dues, she can leave the club without giving up cycling. She can ride her bicycle all by herself. It was her individual choice to cycle that made her a cyclist; belonging to a cycling community was optional, not essential to being a cyclist.

This was basically how I understood salvation—riding your salvation bicycle all by yourself. But it turns out this is a terribly mistaken way of thinking about salvation. The Apostles and Church Fathers would have viewed it as bizarre. Salvation is *not* a private, autonomous, individual, unmediated experience—salvation is being personally gathered by Christ into his salvation community.

The individualistic view of salvation leads to the distinctly Protestant anxiety of having to convince yourself that you are saved. Protestants, with their emphasis on the individual, have no higher authority to confirm their salvation. Instead they must convince themselves they are saved on a purely subjective basis. So they try to "feel saved." But then some emotive evangelist comes along and starts talking about "missing heaven by ten inches" (the distance between head and heart) and the madness begins! "Am I really saved or do I just *think* I'm saved?!" And around and around it goes. I can't tell you how many people I have personally encountered who suffer from crippling mental illness rooted in anxiety over their personal salvation. Some of them even end up in mental institutions suffering deep psychological trauma over the question of whether or not they are saved. But it doesn't have to be this way. Today when I meet someone in this anxious condition, I ask them this— "Do you believe what the church has confessed about Jesus Christ? Do you confess that Jesus Christ is Lord? Have you been baptized?" And if they answer in the affirmative, I tell them, "By the authority of the church I assure you that you belong to the salvation community of Christ." Instead of trying to trust their own erratic feelings, they can trust the testimony of the church that says to them, "You belong to us." It's like citizenship. Citizenship is not based on whether or not you "feel" like a citizen, it's based on what the state says about you. I'm an American citizen because the United States says I am. I am a Christian because the church says I belong to the body of Christ.

What if salvation is better understood as a kind of belonging? It's true that salvation is *personal*, but it's not *individual*. Salvation is communal by design. Human beings are by necessity intensely social—we can survive no other way. Christ establishes and calls us into God's redemptive community. Jesus is the good shepherd who seeks to gather scattered humanity into one flock. Speaking of his gathering work to his fellow Jews, Jesus says, "I have other sheep that do not belong to this fold. I must bring them also, and they will listen to my voice. So there will be one flock, one shepherd" (John 10:16). To be gathered into the flock of Christ is what we mean by salvation. It is a personal experience, but it is inherently communal. Another way of saying it is this: *Salvation is the kingdom of God.*

It's very interesting that Jesus only uses the word "salvation" on two occasions (Luke 19:9, John 4:22). What Jesus talks about almost exclusively is the kingdom of God. Paul on the other hand rarely mentions the kingdom of God, but speaks incessantly on salvation. Here's the point—What Jesus tends to call the kingdom of God, Paul tends to call salvation, *but they are talking about the same thing!* To belong to the redeemed community that lives under the reign and rule of Christ (the kingdom of God) is to enter into the Lord's salvation.

We have grown accustomed to thinking that the Old Covenant is a covenant based on works, while the New Covenant is based on grace. We think the Old Covenant is legalism and the New Covenant is grace. This is almost entirely false. The Jewish people living under the Covenant of Sinai and the Law of Moses were keenly aware that their sins were forgiven by the grace and mercy of God and not by the merit of their works. The difference between the two covenants is not law and grace. The essential difference between the old and new covenants is this—The New Covenant invites *the whole world* to become God's people. In Christ the chosen people are now the human race and the holy land is the whole earth. The Torah that was made obsolete with the arrival of the New Covenant provides the regulations intended to mark out cultural and ethnic boundaries—dietary restrictions, purity codes, ethnic markers, circumcision rituals, and holy days. Instead of being defined by ethnicity, circumcision, and Torah observance, the people of God are now defined by faith, baptism, and obedience to Messiah. The opportunity to belong to the community of salvation is now open to the whole world—which was God's intention all along! The covenant that began with Abraham and Moses culminated in Christ. In Christ the nations are invited to join God's new covenant, new household, new temple, new Israel, new humanity. (These are all terms Paul uses in his epistles to describe the community of salvation.) The "new thing" about the New Covenant is that it erases all ethnic, gender, social, political, and class privilege:

> Neither the Left "do your own thing" nor the Right "do your own thing" is compatible with the "love your neighbor as yourself" ethic of Christ.

> For in Christ you are all children of God through faith. As many of you as were baptized into Christ have clothed yourselves with Christ. There is no longer Jew or Greek, there is no longer slave or free, there is no longer male and female; for all are one in Christ. (Galatians 3:26–28)

Salvation is a kind of belonging! A belonging that was restricted in the Old Covenant, but has now been opened wide in the New Covenant. This is how Jesus and the Apostles thought about salvation. So, on the day of Pentecost, Peter exhorted the people to "save yourselves from this corrupt generation." How? By believing in Jesus, being baptized, and being added to the salvation community that is the church. It is only in modern times that we have begun to think of salvation in terms of individualism. In modernity, the perception of salvation began to warp into a mostly private experience. "Accepting Jesus into your heart" began to replace belonging to the body of Christ. All of this was in keeping with the modern emphasis on "me." The fourth word—"Community"—provided an important course correction in the basic way I viewed Christianity. "Me" would be replaced with "We."

An emphasis on the word "community" helped me understand that if the Jesus we follow doesn't lead us into the community of other followers, we are following a mostly made-up Jesus, a manufactured Jesus designed to accommodate the modern cult of "me." American author Tom Wolfe called the 1970s the "Me Decade"—except that it's now turning into the "Me Half Century." This is the true lasting legacy of the 1960s. "Do your own thing" won the day for both the Left and the Right. Both sides are obsessed with individual rights. The Left doesn't want the government interfering with rights pertaining to abortion, drugs, and marriage. The Right doesn't want the government interfering with rights of gun ownership, a free market, and the utilization of the environment. With both the Left and the Right, individualism has triumphed over a vision for shared wellbeing. Neither the Left "do your own thing" nor the Right "do your own thing" is compatible with the "love your neighbor as yourself" ethic of Christ. Marxism emphasizes collectivism. Capitalism emphasizes individualism. Christianity emphasizes community. Christianity endorses personhood—the inherent worth and dignity of every person. Each person has infinite worth because each person is infinitely loved by God. What Christianity repudiates is the selfishness of individualism. A Christianity that understands itself as a salvation community can save us from the distinctly modern curse of individualism. Christianity knows that John Donne is right—No man is an island. The Apostles don't call us to "accept Jesus into our heart"—they call us to belong to the body of Christ. As the Desert Fathers were fond of saying, "One Christian is no Christian."

REVOLUTION

You say you want a revolution
Well, you know, we all want to change the world
—The Beatles

During the heady days of the Jesus Movement there was a pervasive conviction among the young people involved that we were part of something revolutionary. Our lives had been radically transformed by Jesus and we wanted to relive the Book of Acts. Church as usual was not an option for us. We weren't interested in being conservative or playing it safe. We carried a strong counterculture ethos. We saw Jesus as a revolutionary and we wanted to be revolutionaries too. We shared much of the theology of conservative evangelicals, but our vibe was decidedly counterculture with our long hair, patched blue jeans, and tie-dyed t-shirts. We preached on the streets, in the bars, and at rock concerts. More significantly we had inherited a distrust of government and a disdain for war from the Vietnam era. We saw a Christian critique of war as being faithful to the revolutionary Jesus of the Sermon on the Mount. We had no interest in serving the political causes of either Republicans or Democrats. We saw Christianity as a revolutionary movement that was incompatible with power-hungry political parties. We wanted to change the world in the name of Jesus; we weren't interested in who was the current resident of the White House or the composition of Congress in the name of politics. But that began to change in the Eighties as we were drawn to the siren call of Jerry Falwell and his Moral Majority. It was the beginning of a turning away from a revolutionary Christianity toward a politicized Christianity complicit with partisan politics. For me it was the beginning of a big mistake.

When I began my pastoral ministry during the rise of the Religious Right, conservative Christians were ready to "take back America for God." Evangelicalism was about to become a voting block. The Moral Majority, the Christian Coalition, and Focus on the Family would all become nationally known organizations galvanizing evangelicals as a political force. "Christian Voter

Guides" would be distributed in evangelical churches across the country. The central issue that initially energized the movement was abortion. Since the Republican Party shared the evangelical view on abortion, evangelicals bought into the entire Republican platform. Eventually, support of gun rights, capital punishment, mandatory sentencing, welfare cuts, increased military spending, covert action in Latin America, and the invasion of Iraq came to be regarded as the "Christian position." And I went along for the ride.

I shared platforms with Pat Robertson and Dick Cheney. Senators John Ashcroft and Jim Talent spoke in my church. We handed out those voter guides. We learned to be pro-life and pro-war—and never saw the stunning incongruity! But all of that came to an abrupt end for me in 2004. The epiphany came when I was sitting, of all places, on a platform with Dick Cheney at a campaign rally. I suddenly realized I was nothing more than a puppet in a high-stakes game of power politics. I was being used. I was being asked to exploit the name of Jesus to endorse some politicians. It was a Damascus Road moment for me. "Brian, Brian, why are you politicizing me?" Like Saul of Tarsus I saw the light and was converted. I couldn't exit the arena fast enough. My exit from that campaign rally in 2004 was my exit from the Religious Right. I was on my way to finding something truly revolutionary. I was discovering that the revolution of Christ is the radical alternative to the unimaginative politicism of the religious Right and Left.

It's not that Jesus is apolitical. Far from it. Jesus is *intensely* political! But Jesus has his own politics—and they cannot be made to serve the interests of some other political agenda. As Eugene Peterson says, "The gospel of Jesus Christ is more political than anyone imagines, but in a way that no one guesses."[3] The politics of Jesus are set forth in the Sermon on the Mount—and neither the Republican nor the Democratic party have any intention of seriously adopting those politics! They simply cannot. The politics of the Sermon on the Mount are antithetical to the political interests of a military and economic superpower. The problem with both the Christian Right and the Christian Left is that they reduce "Christian" to the diminished role of religious adjective in service to the all-important political noun. But as Karl Barth taught us, God cannot serve some other interest, God can only rule.

The revolution that is intended is the revolution that occurs when we seriously begin to live under the reign and rule of Christ. The kingdom of Christ is the most revolutionary politics—perhaps the only truly revolutionary politics—the world has ever seen. Unlike all other political agendas, the supreme value of the politics of Jesus is not power, but love. Jesus rejects the politics of power for the politics of love. The politics of Jesus is without coercion. The kingdom of God persuades by love, witness, Spirit, reason, rhetoric, and if need be, martyrdom—but never by force. Conventional politics is a contest to gain the use of coercive force. But Jesus rejects this method. In the politics of Jesus the world will be changed by non-coercive love or not at all. It's not the task of the church to change the world by legislative force. It's the task of the church to be the world changed by Christ. This is revolutionary in a way that conventional politics never can be.

Evangelicalism's participation in the "culture wars" has been an absolute disaster. It was destined to be a disaster from the beginning, because from the outset evangelicals conformed to the conventional assumptions of power politics. With a naïveté that was breathtaking, evangelical Christians thought that Christlikeness in a culture could be achieved by coercive legislation and the American electoral process. It began with Jerry Falwell's Moral Majority and it culminated in the controversial presidency of George W. Bush. Was it worth it? Was it worth transforming "evangelical" from someone who believes in a personal experience with Jesus Christ to a synonym for a petulant Republican? Of course it wasn't worth it! The only positive thing that can come from the experience with the culture wars is to learn this bitter lesson: adopting the means of partisan power politics is an abject betrayal of the revolutionary way of Jesus. We don't need to change the world. Not like that. Not by coercion. Not by trying to heap blame and shame on half the population. Not by legislative force. Trying to change the world by coercive force is not changing the world; it's simply reconfiguring the structures of power. If we are going to attempt something as grand as "changing the world" at all, we do so by being that part of the world changed by Christ. *That's* the revolution we can believe in!

> The politics of Jesus is without coercion. The kingdom of God persuades by love, witness, Spirit, reason, rhetoric, and if need be, martyrdom—but never by force.

"Pro-life" (as a guiding principle and not an empty slogan) is an excellent way to go about identifying the politics of Jesus. Followers of Jesus should be for all that tends toward life and against all that colludes with death. Which is why I'm opposed to the death-friendly practices of abortion, capital punishment, torture, war, predatory capitalism, environmental exploitation, unchecked proliferation of guns, neglecting the poor, refusing the immigrant, and keeping healthcare unaffordable to millions. But even with these pro-life issues I'm not focusing on the coercive means of legislation, but witnessing to the politics of Jesus. It's enough for the church to embody the ethics of Christ. The church doesn't need to enforce this revolution, the church only needs to live it. To those who will dare to adopt the politics of the Sermon on the Mount, Jesus says, "You are the light of the world. A city built upon a hill cannot be hid" (Matthew 5:14). This revolution is nothing like the American Revolution with its musket-toting minutemen or the French Revolution with its bloody guillotines. This revolution was played out in the Book of Acts as small bands of people learned to live under the revolutionary reign of Jesus Christ, so much so that it was said of them, "These people who have been turning the world upside down have come here also…They are all acting contrary to the decrees of the emperor, saying that there is another king named Jesus" (Acts 17:6–7). That's the revolution we are to belong to!

* * *

Today at Word of Life things feel revolutionary again. Like they did back in the Catacombs. (I mean the Catacombs coffeehouse in St. Joseph in the 1970s…but, who knows, maybe even a tiny bit like *the* catacombs of ancient Rome.) I like that. I began my journey with Jesus as a revolutionary Christian and the revolutionary aspects of discipleship may be what I most needed to recover after being domesticated by a conservatism committed to maintaining the status quo. But this also means our message feels a bit dangerous. We talk about Jesus and the kingdom of God in a way that doesn't seem safe. Because we make it clear there is no easy fit between the American way and the Jesus way, we make people uneasy. And people made uneasy with their assumptions can become angry and lash out. So sometimes we have to put up with rumors and innuendos directed our way—subtle or not so subtle suggestions that we have abandoned the faith. Of course, what we have done is to abandon an Americanized faith in search of an apostolic faith. And because an apostolic faith is characterized by the radical forgiveness of Jesus, we forgive our detractors and press on. It can be painful enduring the sting of undeserved criticism, but it's worth it. It's worth enduring some pain to find the Cana where Jesus is still turning water into wine.

Five words. Cross. Mystery. Eclectic. Community. Revolution. Five words given to me when I prayed, "Jesus, tell me what to say." Five words that became signposts to lead me out of the dead-end cul-de-sac I was stuck in. Five words that when put together became a kind of alchemy for turning watered down Americanized Christianity into the robust wine of revolutionary Christianity.

Chapter 3

Three Dreams

"Your young men shall see visions and your old men shall dream
dreams."
—The Prophet Joel

"You may say that I'm a dreamer..."
—John Lennon

I dreamed I was in New York City lost amid the looming
skyscrapers and the kinetic energy of Manhattan. I was on a
quest—I was searching for the faith of Abraham. I
approached people on the streets—policemen, street-
vendors, strangers. "Excuse me, but have you seen the faith of
Abraham?" No one seemed to regard this as a peculiar question,
but each responded matter of factly that they had not. As I
continued my search I became aware of a large crowd of people all
moving in the same direction. I joined the crowd and eventually
thousands of us made our way into an enormous arena where a
Christian event of some sort was taking place. There was

contemporary worship music and revivalist preaching. It was a familiar scene to me. But an instinct told me I wouldn't find the faith of Abraham in the big Christian event. I left the arena to continue my quest. I began to wander into quieter streets. Eventually I found a quaint bookstore nestled in a side street. It was the kind of store where a little bell rang when you opened the door. It had the distinctive smell of old books. It seemed no one was there. It felt vaguely mysterious. I began to browse among the bookshelves, progressively moving toward the back of the store.

When I reached the very back…there sat Abraham himself! He looked like the Jewish rabbi and theologian Abraham Joshua Heschel with his long white beard. But in my dream he was Abraham the patriarch. He was sitting in a big leather chair with piles of prayer books scattered around the floor. He had tears in his eyes. Many of these prayer books were in poor condition. The old man looked at me with a sad smile and said, "I understand you've been looking for my faith." When I said yes, he invited me to sit with him. We had a long conversation. We talked about prayer and especially about prayer books. At the end of our conversation he gave me a kiss. And I woke up.

A few nights later I had another dream. I dreamed I was in Zurich shopping for shoes with the Swiss theologian Karl Barth. (I have, in fact, shopped for shoes in Zurich…but not with Karl Barth—he died when I was nine years old.) While trying on shoes we were holding a lively conversation. The conversation bounced back and forth between theology and shoes. I was asking the great theologian to clarify his doctrine of election. It went something like this, "So Karl, if I understand you correctly, you're saying that all of God's purposes of election are fulfilled in Jesus Christ. Am I getting that right? And what do you think of these shoes? Do you think I should buy this pair or the other ones?" Karl was happy to answer my questions on election and footwear. In my dream I was thinking, "Man! I'm shopping for shoes with Karl Barth and having a great time!" I was both aware and surprised at how comfortable I felt. Here I was with the man widely regarded as the greatest theologian of the twentieth century and we were shopping for shoes and palling around like we were the best of friends. At Karl's recommendation I bought a pair of Ballys. This was a fun dream. And I woke up.

A little later I had the third in my series of dreams. This time I dreamed I was in Calcutta. I've been to India more than a dozen times and the cacophony of sights, sounds, and smells that are unique to India was vivid in my dream. I was riding in a taxi with Mother Teresa. She was sitting on my right. I was surprised at how tiny she was. She was talking with me about the absolute necessity for humility in prayer. Though she spoke kindly to me, I was completely intimidated by this little nun. Her holiness was so otherworldly that I couldn't help but be a little afraid of her. As comfortable as I had been with Karl Barth, I was just as nervous around Mother Teresa. I was very conscious of not wanting to say anything presumptuous or flippant. We would not be shopping for shoes together. We were in the taxi because we were looking for a place to pray. I was in Calcutta to pray with this great saint, but we needed to find a quiet place to pray. The noise and busyness of the city were not conducive to prayer. We were in search of a sacred place. At one point during our taxi ride I wondered where we were. As we passed through a busy intersection I looked out the window and caught a glimpse of the street sign. The sign read, Self Help Avenue. We could not pray there. And I woke up.

Three dreams. New York, Calcutta, Zurich. Father Abraham, Mother Teresa, Karl Barth. Were these dreams significant for me? Very much so! Were these dreams from God? That might be to put too fine a point on it. I would rather say they were dreams about the God-inspired journey I was on—they were part of the ongoing conversation between God and myself about moving beyond a watered-down Americanized Christianity and finding something better. These dreams were creative metaphors depicting my own spiritual and theological quest. They were "water to wine" dreams,

> Modern man has sold his soul for convenience and technology. Faith, serious thought, and prayer are not easily cultivated in the transient and trivial atmosphere of modern mass culture.

dream theater symposiums. Let me suggest what I was seeing and trying to learn in those three dreams.

All three of these dreams were set in big cities—big cities that seemed to represent the frenzied and chaotic nature of modernity. It should be self-evident that the pace, pressure and distractions of modern life are not conducive to a healthy development of the human soul. Modern man has sold his soul for convenience and technology. Faith, serious thought, and prayer are not easily cultivated in the transient and trivial atmosphere of modern mass culture. Everything is a bit too fast, too loud, too superficial. The pressure and pandemonium of contemporary culture was the backdrop in all three dreams.

So there I was in New York City looking for the faith of Abraham—the faith that was pioneered by a man who never moved any faster than the speed of a camel and lived most of his life as a desert nomad. Abraham lived in tents. He was acquainted with quiet and solitude; he knew the darkness of the night. Without the light pollution of modern civilization Abraham could see the stars. He could wonder. He could try to count the stars and discover they are beyond counting. He could muse on these things and conclude that God's promise is beyond measure. He could sense the beauty of the Infinite.

Abraham is called the father of faith, though he may never have known or used the word "faith." Faith was for Abraham what water is for a fish. Faith was the world Abraham inhabited, it was the air he breathed. For Abraham faith was not an abstract concept that could be dissected and analyzed—faith was simply his mysterious and sometimes difficult friendship with the invisible Creator called Yahweh. Abraham walked with God. We call it faith. We name it; Abraham lived it. Abraham's faith was not a "thing" apart from Abraham himself. Abraham's faith was not a means to something else—it was the end itself. His faith was his lived relationship with the living God. Abraham's faith was not a "business contract" with the Omnipotent; it was a real friendship. The friendship itself was its own reward.

I was in New York City, the epicenter of modern capitalism, looking for the kind of faith Abraham lived—a faith that was not a means to an end, but the thing itself. Faith as relationship and not agenda, faith that was not leverage with God, but an orientation of the soul toward God. Faith as love and not power. Faith as friendship and not commodity. Wall Street would indeed be a strange place to look for that kind of faith! But that's what I was doing in my dream. I was asking everyone I met where I could find the faith of Abraham. The peculiar thing was that people seemed to know what I was talking about—what they didn't know was where to find it. Maybe that's the way it is. Deep down inside, don't we at least suspect we are really made for shared relationship and not competitive acquisition? I think we do know this. But we're thrown into a modern world where identity and purpose are almost entirely based in a ruthless contest for status and stuff. Without a primary orientation of the soul toward God, life gets reduced to the pursuit of power and the acquisition of things. Attempting to yoke God to that kind of agenda is what the Bible calls idolatry—God harnessed as means, the holy reduced to utility. It's what Abraham left Ur to get away from. It's what I was trying to get away from.

who says?

At one point in the dream I found myself following the crowd—which rarely is the way to go—and being led into a big Christian conference. It had all the things Americans like best—it was big, loud, exciting, and most of all "practical." The worship was entertaining. The sermons were "applicable to your life." What was being offered were things that you could "use." I knew this world well. But the faith of Abraham was not found there. So I left.

> Without a primary orientation of the soul toward God, life gets reduced to the pursuit of power and the acquisition of things.

It doesn't take the dream interpretation skills of Daniel to get the point. I was in the process of leaving modern pragmatic agenda-based Christianity ...but for what?

Back outside I began to take streets less traveled, quieter streets. That's where I found the bookstore. The difference between the raucous conference and the quiet bookstore could not have been more striking. A few years ago I found a used bookstore in Vancouver that was very much like the one in my dream. Tall shelves with narrow aisles that made you feel like you were in a maze made of books. In the back of the store of my dream, still searching for Abraham's faith, I found Abraham himself—sitting among piles of old prayer books with tears in his eyes. He knew what I was looking for. He talked to me about faith as prayer. But it was a different kind of prayer than I had known—it wasn't agenda-based prayer. It wasn't prayer as a form of God-management. It wasn't prayer as a practical tool. It wasn't acquisitive prayer. It was prayer as faith itself—the orientation of the soul toward God. This was prayer for properly forming the human soul.

In my dream Abraham (in the guise of Rabbi Heschel) explained to me that the faith I was looking for could only be found in prayer, but it was the kind of prayer I knew little about. This is why I needed prayer books. I needed the ancient wisdom of the saints and sages who knew how to pray well. I needed the well-crafted prayers of the historic church to properly form my soul. What I could not find in the conferences and conventions of Christian pop culture, I would find in the practice of prayer shaped by neglected prayer books. This is what Abraham explained to me. His kiss was his blessing. Soon after that dream I began to explore the use of prayer books. It changed my life.

So what about my dream of shopping for shoes with Karl Barth in Zurich? This is the easiest dream to understand. It was about trying on some new theological shoes and finding out I was quite comfortable in them. In the dream I was surprisingly relaxed around the great Swiss theologian—discussing theology and trying on shoes. Soon I would discover I could be comfortable trying on some serious theology. I began to try on the theological shoes of Barth and Bonhoeffer, Wright and Brueggemann, Yoder and

Hauerwas, Jürgen Moltmann and Miroslav Volf, David Bentley Hart and William T. Cavanaugh...and I found some good fits. This was wonderful because the fundamentalist footwear was really beginning to pinch. I couldn't walk in those shoes anymore. In my past trajectory from the Jesus movement to the charismatic movement to the word of faith movement, I had few encounters with serious theology. The circles in which I traveled had a general disinterest, if not disdain, for real theology. But I had now been reading philosophy, the Church Fathers, and classic literature for several years, and that kind of smug anti-intellectual approach to thinking about God held no interest for me. If I was going to think and speak about God—which is what theology is and what pastors do!—it was time to take it seriously.

2004 was a year of intense spiritual journey. I was devouring books, mostly theology. One of the few non-theological books I read that year was *Chronicles*—the newly published autobiography by Bob Dylan. In this dreamy memoir Dylan recounts how a hunger for knowledge was first kindled in his soul. It was 1961 and Dylan was a twenty-year old unknown coffeehouse singer. From time to time he stayed in the apartment of a New York intellectual who had a substantial personal library. Here's how Dylan recalls the first time he saw this library:

> I cut the radio off, crisscrossed the room, pausing
> for a moment, to turn on the black-and-white TV.
> *Wagon Train* was on. It seemed to be beaming in
> from some foreign country. I shut that off, too,
> and went into the other room, a windowless one
> with a painted door—a dark cavern with a floor

> to ceiling library. I switched on the lamps. The
> place had an overpowering presence of literature
> and you couldn't help but lose your passion for
> dumbness.[1]

"Lose your passion for dumbness." I underlined those words. It became a kind of personal maxim. I would say, "Brian, it's time to lose your passion for dumbness." It was time to switch off *Wagon Train*—or whatever—and settle into the library. And I did. What I discovered was that serious-minded, praying people had been thinking about the God revealed in Christ and writing about it for two thousand years. They had important things to say. Thinkers and theologians, reformers and revivalists like Athanasius, Augustine, Aquinas, Erasmus, Luther, Wesley had all made their important contributions. But the conversation that is Christian theology is ongoing. Contemporary theologians are making important contributions today—and I decided I wanted to be in on that conversation. The price for being a participant was to become conversant on what the church had already said about the Triune God. It's what we call Christian theology.

Please be careful about saying things like, "I don't care about theology, I'm just into Jesus." I want to say, "What Jesus?" The moment you begin to try to answer that question you are doing theology—it's just a matter of whether or not you'll do it well. Yes, I understand we can't have a purely academic approach to theology— our best theologians *all* agree with that. Prayer and theology go together! The fact is, if we are going to think and talk about God, we can't avoid theology, and what we're doing is important enough to warrant our finest minds attending to it. Most Christians aren't going to be trained theologians—just like most Christians aren't going to be pastors. But we need pastors and we need theologians. To belittle the work of the theologian is to advocate a spiritual poverty. We need more than Christian folk religion—we need a Christianity that is serious and substantive in its thought.

Inquiry into the nature of God (theology) is what used to be called the "queen of the sciences." If physics deserves an Albert Einstein, then theology deserves a Karl Barth. I'll never be able to produce something like Barth's *Dogmatics* and it remains an open question whether I'll ever get around to reading all *six million words* of this voluminous work! But I know it's important and I deeply appreciate a brilliant and devout theologian giving his life to helping us think correctly about our Christian faith. The ongoing quest to articulate the revelation of God in Christ is worthy of humanity's continued best effort. What Newton said about physics was a huge advancement. But physics didn't end with Newton. Einstein came along and gave humanity a breakthrough in how we understand the cosmos. Likewise, what Thomas Aquinas accomplished in his *Summa Theologica* in the thirteenth century was enormously important. But theology didn't end with Aquinas. In the twentieth century Karl Barth came along and gave us a breakthrough with his *Dogmatics*. Christian theology is the church's ongoing conversation about the revelation of the Word of God who is Jesus Christ. At its best, theology is an act of worship—it is the act of loving God with all our mind.

Of course all Christians are not expected to be theologians any more than all people are expected to be scientists. But just because not everyone can or will become a scientist doesn't mean scientific inquiry is unimportant. We can say the same thing about theologians. The vast majority of Christians aren't even going to be "armchair theologians." They don't need to be. But all Christians need to be taught by teachers and pastors who take theology seriously. American Christianity has far too many pastors who will read business journals and leadership books but can't be bothered to take theology seriously. In the context of juvenile pop Christianity, theology is irrelevant and unwanted. Many congregations suffer as a result...and they don't even know it.

One of the sad things about spiritual poverty is that the impoverished hardly ever know they're suffering from it. If you're going to be a teaching pastor you owe it to your congregation to be able to speak in an intelligent and orthodox manner upon your subject. Like Bob Dylan said, lose your passion for dumbness. Or perhaps I can say it more politely. Theological ignorance may not be a sin, but it's not a virtue, and it's certainly not something to boast about! The American church

> As long as we control the agenda, prayer will be seen as a means of manipulating Omnipotence to our advantage— which is a fair description of idolatry.

would benefit greatly from a renaissance of theologically informed preaching. Thankfully there are signs that just such a renaissance may be underway among a new generation of young pastors.

After my nighttime visitations to New York and Zurich to converse with two men, I had one more appointment to keep. This time I would meet a woman—Mother Teresa. As Ebenezer Scrooge feared the third specter most of all, I found my "visit" with the saint of Calcutta a bit unnerving. With no preliminaries in the dream I was suddenly riding in a taxi with Mother Teresa. We were looking for a place to pray. As we rode together she talked to me about prayer. I just listened. I never spoke a word. She was stressing the necessity of absolute humility in prayer. The only thing I did in the dream was to look out the window to see where we were. The street sign read Self Help Avenue…and I knew we couldn't pray there. This dream seemed to literally spell out its most important lesson—as long as we travel the road of self-help we will never really be able to pray.

In my dream I was nervous around Mother Teresa. In real life many a head of state was more than a little nervous meeting the famous nun from Albania. Roles were reversed for these international movers and shakers in a way they were unaccustomed to. The sweaty palm now belonged to the powerbroker politicians. There is a comedy of the absurd to be seen in this—not unlike the comedy of Revelation where a little lamb triumphs over vicious beasts. In Mother Teresa we find a humble woman who possessed nothing commensurate with conventional power. Yet presidents and prime ministers of superpowers were obviously intimidated by this little nun whose authority flowed from her holy otherness. Standing completely outside the game of power politics, her apostolic poverty gave her a unique authority—an authority the principalities and powers could not comprehend and thus found intimidating. My friend Jason Upton wrote a song inspired by this phenomenon in Mother Teresa's life—he calls the song, appropriately, "Poverty."

> There's a power in poverty that breaks principalities
> And brings the authorities down to their knees
> And there's a brewing frustration and ageless temptation
> To fight for control by some manipulation

But the God of the kingdoms and God of the nations
And God of creation sends this revelation
Through the homeless and penniless Jesus the Son
The poor will inherit the kingdom to come
And where will we turn when our world falls apart
And all of the treasures we've stored in our barns
Can't buy the kingdom of God

And who will we praise when we've praised all our lives
Men who build kingdoms and men who build fame
But heaven does not know their names

And what will we fear when all that remains
Is God on the throne with a child in his arms
And love in his eyes
And the sound of his heart cry

Humility, poverty, and prayer—this has always been the open secret of the saints. It's the very opposite of the self-help agenda that drives Christian marketing today. We are endlessly tempted to place prayer in the uniquely modern category of self-help. But true prayer is no such thing. Prayer is not a "technique" for making our lives "better" as understood by the assumed cultural values of consumerist America. Neither is prayer something we can be in charge of. As long as we control the agenda, prayer will be seen as a means of manipulating Omnipotence to our advantage—which is a fair description of idolatry. We make a huge mistake when we see prayer as a technique for getting God to do what we want him to do. This is basically how prayer is marketed in the pop Christian world, but it's a sham. The kind of prayer Mother Teresa spoke to me about in the Calcutta taxi dream is nothing like that. Mother Teresa's approach to prayer involves a deep cultivation of humility and poverty of spirit, which is why genuine prayer is so unmarketable. Franciscan priest Richard Rohr stresses this when he says:

> Prayer is unmarketable. Prayer gives you no immediate payoff. You get no immediate feedback or sense of success. True prayer, in that sense, probably is the most courageous and countercultural thing an American will ever do.[2]

We need prayer that is countercultural instead of culturally conformed. We can't honestly pray on Self Help Avenue. That kind of praying is not really prayer at all—it's trying to take God shopping. My dream was telling me I needed to rescue my prayer life from the distortions of American self-help agendas. In my first and third dreams Father Abraham and Mother Teresa were saying much the same thing and I was coming to have a whole new perspective on prayer. Abandoning a self-help agenda in prayer for the spiritual formation that can occur through the use of the great prayer books of the church was having a huge influence on me. Today my understanding and practice of prayer is radically different than it was ten years ago, and, as a result, I am a markedly different person than I was ten years ago. For that I am grateful. True prayer is found, not on Self Help Avenue, but in the sacred space of Christian liturgy. The quiet place where ego agenda can die and a new humility can be born.

* * *

Those were my three dreams. Dreams of direction, correction, and encouragement—the charity of night. Dreams are a mysterious thing. The ability to take desire and longing, fear and loathing and weave them into nocturnal narratives is one of the most remarkable aspects of the human soul. I think this is the best way to understand my three dreams. I was struggling to make sense of my spiritual journey during waking hours, so in my dreams I reached out to a Hebrew patriarch, a Protestant theologian, and a Catholic nun who could give me some direction and articulate what I needed to hear. I needed to be steered toward the ancient wisdom of praying with prayer books. I needed to bid a final farewell to the noisy avenues of self-help Christianity. I needed someone to encourage me to continue my quest for substantive theology. I found the help I needed in dreamland. Thank you, Father Abraham. Thank you, Mother Teresa. Thank you, Brother Barth. You came to me when I needed you most. Was it all just a dream or something more? Who knows? Like I said, dreams are a mysterious thing.

We are such stuff
As dreams are made on;
And our little life
Is rounded with a sleep.
—Shakespeare, *The Tempest*

Chapter 4

Jerusalem Bells

My "three dreams" provided helpful guidance—like when we used to stop at a gas station in a strange town to ask for directions. The things they pointed me toward began to influence my new spiritual direction. In my mysterious dreamland encounters both Father Abraham and Mother Teresa spoke to me about prayer. I'm sure it's significant that two of my three turning-point dreams had to do with prayer. I'm tempted to try to make an equation out of this and say that two thirds of our spiritual formation depends on how we pray. That's probably true, but since I'm not fond of spiritual formulas I'll just say that the most important factor in my second half of life journey has involved learning how to pray well.

Part of my learning to pray well has involved reclaiming the frowned-upon word "religious." There is no denying that the word "religious" has fallen into increasing disfavor in modern times.

Most twenty-first century Westerners are very reluctant to identify themselves as religious. But this is a mistake. We have surrendered to the Enlightenment's assault upon religion. We have saluted Voltaire and Nietzsche—even Christians. Today the insipid mantra is "I'm not religious, I'm spiritual." The idea is that the "spiritual" person has transcended the hidebound strictures of what is dismissed with a sneer as "organized religion." To be "spiritual" is acceptable. To be religious is not. But the "I'm-not-religious-but-spiritual" motto is really just a modern rejection of time-tested wisdom in favor of a make-it-up-as-you-go approach. The assumption is that each person's approach to the development of a healthy spiritual life is as valid as any other. The dogma of vague spirituality is that we are all capable of properly forming our spiritual lives as private individuals independent of any received tradition. Of course this is all nonsense. It's analogous to a ten-year-old watching reruns of *Kung Fu* and thinking he has mastered the martial arts! Children flailing about in pajamas may be an entertaining way to pass a Saturday morning but it shouldn't be confused with actually learning kung fu. And neither should boutique "spirituality" be confused with the practices that have been historically identified with Christian spiritual formation.

In keeping with what I consider a penchant for a healthy dose of rebellion, I unabashedly call myself religious. Self-identifying as a religious person may be one of the last acts of rebellion possible in our libertine era! In the secular West, the religious person may be the last rebel. So let me say it deliberately and with a hint of defiance: *I'm not just spiritual, I'm religious.* Anyone can be spiritual. Atheists are spiritual these days! So of course I'm spiritual—we all are!—but I am also intentionally religious. I accept the rigors and disciplines of a religious tradition. I do so because I refuse to leave my spiritual formation to the fads of amorphous "spirituality." I confess sacred creeds and observe a sacred calendar. Most of all I'm a religious person because I pray. Prayer is what religious people do. In that sense I have a solidarity with all who pray. I have more in common with the Egyptian Muslim who prays five times a day than with the European secularist who never prays. I have more in common with the Indian Hindu who prays to Brahma than with the American consumerist who prays to no one at all. I have more in common with the mystic Rumi than with the Deist Jefferson. (That the majority of American evangelicals feel more at home with an Enlightenment secularist than with a Muslim mystic shows just how secular we really are!)

> We are formed as Christian people as we learn the regular rhythms of praying well-crafted, theologically-sound, time-tested prayers.

But neither am I just generically religious. I am specifically and intentionally Christian. The creeds I confess and the calendar I observe are Christian. I pray as a Christian. I pray to the God who is Father, Son, and Holy Spirit. I pray in the name of Jesus Christ. I pray the prayer Jesus gave his disciples to pray. I pray the prayers of historic Christianity. How we pray is how we are formed. The Hindu is formed by Hindu prayers. The Jew is formed by Jewish prayers. The Christian is formed by Christian prayers. The Muslim is formed by Muslim prayers. The secularist is formed by not praying. The "spiritual-but-not-religious" person is formed by only praying whatever and whenever they feel like praying without any respect for a received tradition of prayer. They are essentially secularists sporting a spiritual accessory—whether they know it or not.

Those who hold to the idea that "the only authentic prayers are my own prayers" are scrupulously following the dictates of Voltaire and Jefferson in rejecting the authority of religious tradition. They have endorsed Voltaire's cynicism and Jefferson's scissors. Voltaire scorned the church and Jefferson cut up the Bible—and both did so to demonstrate that organized religion should have no authority in the life of a modern person belonging to the Age of Reason. Formative religion was out and all that remained was nebulous spirituality. This is the origin of the "spiritual but not religious person." If they pray at all, they will pray their own prayers, which is to say, they are not being formed by prayer, they are only "expressing themselves." They wish for what they want and call it prayer. It's window shopping imagined as prayer. This is the prayer of the consumerist, the secularist, the spiritual individualist. But the church has always known better. Christian tradition knows better. We are formed as Christian people as we learn the regular rhythms of praying well-crafted, theologically-sound, time-tested prayers. And what led me to this deeper understanding of prayer was a most unlikely thing—the Muslim *adhan*.

If you visit the Islamic world you quickly become acquainted with the *adhan*—the Muslim call to prayer. You may very well become acquainted with it at five o'clock in the morning! Five times a day, beginning before sunrise, you hear the cry of the muezzin from the minarets—*Allahu Akbar*. It's a call to prayer. When I first began to travel in the Islamic world I reacted to the Muslim call to prayer with an irritation rooted in cultural disdain and religious triumphalism. I was annoyed by it. I didn't want to hear it. But eventually I began to feel differently. To be honest, I was somewhat envious. Here was a culture with a public call to prayer. In the secular, post-Christian West we have nothing like this. The best we can manage is to clandestinely bow our heads for ten seconds in a restaurant and hope no one notices. We don't call people to prayer. Few Christians living outside of monasteries pray five times a day. We pray whenever we feel like it…and too much of the time we don't feel like it. But in the Islamic world I found a religious culture that publicly called people to prayer five times a day! I was envious of a society that held to a religious tradition where prayer was taken seriously and attended to in a prescribed manner. So when I heard the *adhan* I would wistfully think, I wish we had something like that. Then one day the pieces fell into place.

I was walking through the cobblestone streets of the Old City of Jerusalem on a Sunday morning when I began to hear the bells toll—church bells. A cacophony of sacred sound centuries old. Orthodox bells, Catholic bells, Anglican bells, Lutheran bells. The enormous bells from the Church of the Holy Sepulchre seemed to belong to another age. It was a wonder I found strangely moving. That's when it dawned on me—this is the Christian *adhan*. Church bells are the Christian call to prayer. (A practice predating the Muslim *adhan* by centuries.) Of course I knew this, but had somehow forgotten it. I had forgotten the bells just as the post-Christian West has forgotten the bells.

The small town Baptist church I grew up in had, like all churches in those days, a bell. A cadre of old men were in charge of ringing it on Sunday mornings. When I was a small child they would occasionally let me "help" ring the bell. I would hold onto the rope reaching into the belfry and as the bell began to toll I would be pulled up off my feet. The old men would laugh. It's a fond memory. But a faded memory. Somewhere along the way church bells began to disappear. They became antiquated. We moved to the suburbs, built our new nondescript utilitarian metal buildings and left the bells behind. Church bells have become passé. The more contemporary the church the less likely that it has a bell. This is a sad and apropos harbinger.

In a poetic sense the sound of Islam is the *adhan*. The sound of Hinduism is the *om*. The sound of Buddhism is the *dungchen*. The sound of Judaism is the *shofar*. The sound of Christianity is the church bell. The sound of the post-Christian secular West is the sad dearth of the church bell. The church in the West is no longer public or prayerful. We are now private. The only way we know how to be public is to be political. It's a tragedy that the dominant expression of public Christianity in America over the past generation has been one of political partisanship. My critique of this is not a call to quietism, but a call to transcend crass political rhetoric and bring a prophetic message from elsewhere.   The church bell is a good metaphor of how the church *should* be public. The ringing of a church bell is a public act, but it's not a political act. The church bell is a public call to prayer. The question is, can the American church once again be known as a praying community? I hope so. I long for our public presence to be more like the beauty of tolling church bells and less like the shrillness of haranguing political ads.

A few years ago I started saying among our leadership team that we needed a bell. Churches should have bells. Then I heard how much bells cost! I had no idea they were so expensive. So I set the idea aside until an act of providence made a bell possible. Our administrator found an old bell recovered from an abandoned country church. We installed it on the roof of our modern building and rang it for the first time at a special service marking the beginning of Advent. It's a humble bell. It doesn't have a big sound. It's mostly a symbolic gesture. But I love it. It's a small act of resistance in the age of secularism—a forgotten bell from an abandoned church now back in service, calling the faithful to prayer. I smile when I hear the tolling of our long silenced and now recovered church bell. It seems to be saying all the right things.

The Sunday when I heard the Jerusalem bells I adopted a simple program for prayer during my time in Jerusalem. Whenever I heard the Christian church bell or the Muslim *adhan*, I would stop and pray the Lord's Prayer. My wife and I were leading a Christian pilgrimage at the time and we taught our group this practice. Whenever we heard the five-time-daily *adhan*, we would stop and pray the Lord's Prayer—not as an act of religious one-upmanship, but simply as a Christian response to the call to prayer. Our pilgrim group quickly took to this practice. Our Jewish guide encouraged us. Whenever the *adhan* would sound she would pause and say, "Oh, it's time for you to pray your prayer." And so we would. *Our Father who art in heaven...*

Praying at set times is not a novel innovation but the recovery of an ancient Christian practice. The *Didache*—a late first or early second century manual on Christian practice—instructs believers to pray the Lord's Prayer three times daily. Eventually praying the Lord's Prayer at morning, noon, and night became the practice. By the fifth century, bells were being used to signal these times of prayer.

The episode with the Muslim *adhan* and the Jerusalem bells marked a new beginning in prayer for me. I started praying the hours—or a variation of it. I adopted a schedule of praying morning, noon, evening, night. But what to pray? I prayed the

Lord's Prayer, a psalm, and whatever else came to mind—a humble beginning. But I also began to experiment with prayer books. (After all, this is what Abraham spoke to me about in my dream.) After exploring Catholic, Orthodox, and Anglican prayer books, I

> When it comes to spiritual formation, we are what we pray. Without wise input that comes from outside ourselves, we will never change.

eventually settled on *The Book of Common Prayer* as my primary prayer book. Over a period of a few years, through trial and error, I developed a liturgy of prayer that not only changed my prayer life…it changed me! The key discovery I made had to do with the fundamental purpose of prayer. *The primary purpose of prayer is not to get God to do what we think God ought to do, but to be properly formed.* Prayer is not about advising or managing God; prayer is about being properly formed. If prayer is not a letter to Santa but a practice of spiritual formation, we cannot trust individual spirituality—we need to instead trust the prayers.

> Now Jesus was praying in a certain place, and when he finished, one of his disciples said to him, "Lord, teach us to pray as John taught his disciples." And he said to them, "When you pray, say…" (Luke 11:1– 2, ESV)

When Jesus' disciples asked to be taught how to pray, Jesus didn't give them a theory of prayer or a sentimental aphorism like, "just talk to God." What he did was give them a prayer, which is what his disciples expected. This is what Jewish rabbis did—they composed prayers for their disciples. It was assumed that the way to learn to pray well is to pray prayers composed by a wise teacher. So Jesus said, "When you pray, *say...*" And he gave them a prayer. *You want to know how to pray? Here, pray this.* But those formed in an evangelical tradition have a deep suspicion of what we think of as "prepackaged" prayers. Quite often an evangelical will tell me that Jesus didn't actually intend for us to pray the prayer he gave to us. But of course he did! The evangelical aversion to praying composed prayers—even the Lord's Prayer!—is revealing. What it exposes is our modern arrogance. We want to be in charge of our own praying. So we protest, *how dare someone try to tell me how to pray!* Even if that someone is Jesus!

If we think of prayer as "just talking to God" and that it consists mostly in asking God to do this or that, then we don't need to be given prayers to pray. Just tell God what we want. But if prayer is spiritual formation and not God-management, then we cannot depend on our self to pray properly. If we trust our self to pray, we just end up recycling our own issues—mostly anger and anxiety—without experiencing any transformation. We pray in circles. We pray and stay put. We pray prayers that begin and end in our own little self. When it comes to spiritual formation, we are what we pray. Without wise input that comes from outside ourselves, we will never change. We will just keep praying what we already are. A selfish person prays selfish prayers. An angry person prays angry prayers. A greedy person prays greedy prayers. A manipulative person prays manipulative prayers. Nothing changes. We make no progress. But it's worse than that. Not only do we not make any progress, we actually harden our heart. To consistently pray in a wrong way reinforces a wrong spiritual formation. Richard Rohr says it like this:

As soon as you make prayer a way to get what you want, you're not moving into any kind of new state of consciousness. It's the same old consciousness, but now well disguised: "How can I get God to do what I want God to do?" It's the egocentric self deciding what it needs, but now, instead of just manipulating everybody else, it tries to manipulate God. This is one reason religion is so dangerous and often so delusional. If religion does not transform people at the level of both mind and heart, it ends up giving self-centered people a very pious and untouchable way to be on top and in control. Now God becomes their defense system for their small self![1]

If we are going to pray better, we need better prayers. The Lord's Prayer was composed by the genius of Jesus, and he fully intends for his disciples to pray it as a formative prayer. When you pray, say...

Our Father, who art in heaven,
hallowed be thy Name,
thy kingdom come,
thy will be done,
on earth as it is in heaven.
Give us this day our daily bread.
And forgive us our trespasses,
as we forgive those who trespass against us.
And lead us not into temptation,

but deliver us from evil.
For thine is the kingdom,
and the power, and the glory,
forever. Amen.

We don't just read the Lord's Prayer in the Sermon on the Mount—we pray it! The Lord's Prayer existed as a prayer in the life of the church before it was incorporated into Scripture. Yes, we can use it as an outline for prayer. I do that. But we should also pray it as a complete prayer. It's the perfect prayer. The disciples of Jesus have been praying the Lord's Prayer for nearly two thousand years. It's our prayer of prayers. When we pray the Lord's Prayer, we have prayed well. Among the most eloquent tributes to the Lord's prayer is one from an unexpected source. The atheist-humanist Kurt Vonnegut said:

> While Einstein's theory of relativity may one day put Earth on the intergalactic map, it will always run a distant second to the Lord's Prayer, whose harnessing of energies in their proper, life-giving direction surpasses even the discovery of fire.[2]

The "harnessing of energies in their proper, life-giving direction" is a beautiful way of describing the formative power of the Lord's Prayer. Every time we pray the Lord's Prayer we can be sure we have prayed well and that we have taken another step in the journey toward becoming a properly formed human being. When the first church was being formed in the days following Pentecost, the first Christians devoted themselves to the prayers.

They devoted themselves to the apostles' teaching
and fellowship, to the breaking of bread and *the
prayers*. (Acts 2:42, emphasis added)

The first believers didn't just devote themselves to prayer in an abstract sense, rather they devoted themselves to *the prayers*. If we were told that the church following the day of Pentecost devoted themselves to prayer, we would hear it as a vague, open-ended statement. But we are told that they devoted themselves to *the prayers*. And that's a completely different statement. It's one that almost offends the individualist sensibilities of evangelicals. *You mean they were saying prayers?!* Yes, that's exactly what they were doing. Of course the next question is, what prayers? We're not told, but we can be sure they were praying the Lord's Prayer and the Psalms—the prayer Jesus gave them to pray, and the prayers from the prayer book they already had. The Psalter was (and is) the primary Jewish prayer book. The Psalter was Jesus' prayer book. Jesus prayed the Psalms throughout his life—he even prayed from the Psalms on the cross. "My God, my God, why have you forsaken me?" is the opening line of Psalm 22.

> Liturgy is neither alive nor dead. Liturgy is either true or false. What is alive or dead is the worshiper. So what we need is a true liturgy and a living worshiper.

When we pray the Psalms we are continuing a three-thousand-year-old tradition—a tradition practiced by Jesus and the Apostles. We pray the Psalms, not to express what we feel, but to learn to feel what they express. In praying the Psalms we learn to experience the whole range of human emotion in a way that is healthy and healing. Praying the Psalms may be among the most effective exercises available to us for preserving mental and emotional health.

In their devotion to the prayers, the church was certainly praying the Lord's Prayer and the Psalms. But the church was also beginning to compose its own prayers. This is the origin of what we know as liturgy. And, yes, liturgy is another word evangelicals don't like. But this is unwarranted. Liturgy is a Bible word. It's the Greek word *leitourgeo* and is usually translated as worship or minister. It means "work of the people." The idea is that liturgy is what people do during worship. Worship is not a kind of spiritual entertainment—worship is a work of spiritual formation. The objection I often hear to the use of liturgy—a formal track of worship—is that it's dead. But this is a category mistake. Liturgy is neither alive nor dead. Liturgy is either true or false. What is alive or dead is the worshiper. So what we need is a true liturgy and a living worshiper.

In reality, liturgy cannot be avoided. Every church that worships and every person who prays has a liturgy—it's just a matter of whether or not it's a well-formed liturgy. If I visit your church a couple of Sundays or listen to you pray a few times, I can tell you what your liturgy is—because you definitely have one. It's simply your pattern of worship and prayer. When I enter into prayer, what I want and need is a true track that I can follow. I don't want to depend solely on myself. I want to access the accumulated wisdom of the church in forming a liturgy of prayer. This is the liturgy of morning prayer I've been using and teaching others to use for several years.

A Liturgy for Morning Prayer

Address
Father God, creator of heaven and earth,
God of Abraham, Isaac, and Jacob,
God of Israel,
God and Father of our Lord and Savior Jesus Christ,
True and Living God who is Father, Son, and Holy Spirit,
Have mercy and hear my prayer.

First Prayers
O Lord, open our lips.
And our mouth shall proclaim your praise.

Glory to the Father, and to the Son, and to the Holy Spirit:
as it was in the beginning is now, and will be forever. Amen.
Hallelujah.

O God, make speed to save us.
O Lord, make haste to help us.

Glory to the Father, and to the Son, and to the Holy Spirit:
as it was in the beginning is now, and will be forever. Amen.
Hallelujah.

The Jesus Prayer
Lord Jesus Christ, Son of God, have mercy on me.

Confession of Sin

Most merciful God,
we confess that we have sinned against you
in thought, word, and deed,
by what we have done,
and by what we have left undone.
We have not loved you with our whole heart;
we have not loved our neighbors as ourselves.
We are truly sorry and we humbly repent.
For the sake of your Son Jesus Christ,
have mercy on us and forgive us;
that we may delight in your will,
and walk in your ways,
to the glory of your Name. Amen.

Psalm for the Day

(Corresponding to the day of the year)

Gospel Reading

(According to the Revised Common Lectionary)

Apostles' Creed

I believe in God, the Father almighty,
creator of heaven and earth.
I believe in Jesus Christ, his only Son, our Lord.
He was conceived by the power of the Holy Spirit
and born of the Virgin Mary.
He suffered under Pontius Pilate,
was crucified, died, and was buried.

He descended to the dead.

On the third day he rose again.

He ascended into heaven,

and is seated at the right of the Father.

He will come again to judge the living and the dead.

I believe in the Holy Spirit,

the holy catholic Church,

the communion of the saints,

the forgiveness of sins,

the resurrection of the body,

and the life everlasting. Amen.

Jesus Prayer

Lord Jesus Christ, Son of God, have mercy on me.

Psalm 23

The Lord is my shepherd;

I shall not want.

He makes me lie down in green pastures

He leads me beside still waters.

He restores my soul.

He leads me in paths of righteousness for his Name's sake.

Even though I walk through the valley of the shadow of death,

I shall fear no evil;

For you are with me;

Your rod and your staff, they comfort me.

You prepare a table before me in the presence of my enemies;

You anoint my head with oil,

My cup overflows.

Surely goodness and mercy shall follow me all the days of my life,
and I will dwell in the house of the Lord forever.

Psalm 91:1–2

He who dwells in the secret place of the Most High,
shall abide under the shadow of the Almighty
I will say of the Lord,
"You are my fortress and my refuge,
my God in whom I will trust.

Prayer for Family

Psalm 103:1–5

Bless the Lord, O my soul,
and all that is within me, bless his holy Name.
Bless the Lord, O my soul,
and forget not all his benefits.
He pardons all your iniquities,
and heals all your diseases;
He redeems your life from the pit
and crowns you with lovingkindness and mercy;
He satisfies you with good things,
so that your youth is renewed like the eagle's.
Bless the Lord, O my soul,
And all that is within me bless his holy name.

Lord's Prayer

Our Father, who art in heaven,
hallowed be thy Name,

thy kingdom come,
thy will be done,
on earth as it is in heaven.
Give us this day our daily bread.
And forgive us our trespasses,
as we forgive those who trespass against us.
And lead us not into temptation,
but deliver us from evil.
For thine is the kingdom,
and the power, and the glory,
forever. Amen.

Jesus Prayer
Lord Jesus Christ, Son of God, have mercy on me.

The Lord's Prayer Expanded
Our Father, Holy Father, Abba Father, in the heavens,
Hallowed, holy, sacred be your name.
From the rising of the sun, to the going down of the same,
The name of the Lord is to be praised.
Great is the Lord and greatly to be praised.
Holy, holy, holy is the Lord God of hosts,
The whole earth is full of your glory.
Holy, holy, holy is the Lord God almighty,
Who was and is and is to come.
Thy kingdom come, thy will be done,
On earth as it is in heaven.
Thy government come, thy politics be done,
On earth as it is in heaven.

Thy reign and rule come, thy plans and purposes be done,

On earth as it is in heaven.

May we be an anticipation of the age to come.

May we embody the reign of Christ here and now.

Give us day by day our daily bread.

Provide for the poor among us.

As we seek first your kingdom and your justice,

May all we need be provided for us.

Forgive us our trespasses as we forgive those who trespass against us.

Forgive us our sins as we forgive those who sin against us.

Forgive us our debts as we forgive our debtors.

Transform us by the Holy Spirit into a forgiving community of forgiven sinners.

Lead us not into trouble, trial, tribulation or temptation.

Be mindful of our frame, we are but dust,

We can only take so much.

Lead us out of the wilderness into the promised land that flows with milk and honey,

Lead us out of the badlands into resurrection country.

Deliver us from evil and the evil one.

Save us from Satan, the accuser and adversary.

So that no weapon formed against us shall prosper.

So that every tongue that rises against us in accusation you will condemn.

So that every fiery dart of the wicked one is extinguished by the shield of faith.

So that as we submit to you and resist the devil, the devil flees.

So that as we draw near to Jesus Christ lifted up,

His cross becomes for us the axis of love expressed in forgiveness,

That refounds the world;

And the devil, who became the false ruler of the fallen world,
Is driven out from among us.
For thine is the kingdom and the power and the glory, forever.
Amen

Petition and Intercession
(Making our needs known and praying for others)

Contemplation
(Sitting with Jesus)

Prayer to the Crucified Christ
Lord Jesus, you stretched out your arms of love upon the hard
wood of the cross that everyone might come within the reach of
your saving embrace: So clothe us in your Spirit that we, reaching
forth our hands in love, may bring those who do not know you to
the knowledge and love of you; for the honor of your name. Amen.

The Beatitudes
Blessed are the poor in spirit, for theirs is the kingdom of heaven.
Blessed are those who mourn, for they shall be comforted.
Blessed are the meek, for they shall inherit the earth.
Blessed are those who hunger and thirst for justice, for they shall
be satisfied.
Blessed are the merciful, for they shall receive mercy.
Blessed are the pure in heart, for they shall see God.
Blessed are the peacemakers, for they shall be called the children of God.
Blessed are those who are persecuted for righteousness sake, for
theirs is the kingdom of heaven.

Prayer for Peace

O God, you have made of one blood all the peoples of the earth, and sent your blessed Son to preach peace to those who are far off and to those who are near: Grant that people everywhere may seek after you and find you; bring the nations into your fold; pour out your Spirit upon all flesh; and hasten the coming of your kingdom; through Jesus Christ our Lord. Amen.

Prayer of St. Francis

Lord, make me an instrument of your peace.

Where there is hatred, let me sow love;

Where there is injury, pardon;

Where there is doubt, faith;

Where there is despair, hope;

Where there is darkness, light;

And where there is sadness, joy,

O Divine Master, grant that I may not so much seek to be consoled as to console;

to be understood, as to understand;

to be loved, as to love.

For it is in giving that we receive;

it is in pardoning that we are pardoned;

and it is in dying that we are born to eternal life.

Amen.

Prayer for the Week

(The weekly collect from *The Book of Common Prayer*)

Prayer for Grace

Lord God, almighty and everlasting Father, you have brought us in safety to this new day: preserve us with your mighty power, that we may not fall into sin, nor be overcome by adversity; and in all we do, direct us to the fulfilling of your purpose, through Jesus Christ our Lord. Amen.

Prayer of Thanksgiving

Almighty God, Father of all mercies,
we your unworthy servants give you humble thanks
for all your goodness and lovingkindness
to us and to all whom you have made.
We bless you for our creation, preservation,
and all the blessings of this life;
but above all for your immeasurable love
in the redemption of the world by our Lord Jesus Christ;
for the means of grace, and for the hope of glory.
And, we pray, give us such an awareness of your mercies,
that with truly thankful hearts we may show forth your praise,
not only with our lips, but in our lives,
by giving up our selves to your service,
and by walking before you
in holiness and righteousness all our days;
through Jesus Christ our Lord,
to whom, with you and the Holy Spirit,
be honor and glory throughout all ages. Amen.

Prayer for Mercy

Lord, have mercy.

Christ, have mercy.

Lord, have mercy.

Confession of the Mystery

Christ has died.

Christ is risen.

Christ will come again.

Jesus Prayer

Lord Jesus Christ, Son of God, have mercy on me.

This is the track of prayer I use every morning of my life. It's not a recitation of rote words; it's a liturgy brimming with life. It's not empty; it's full of sacred truth. It's not dry; it's as fresh as the Holy Spirit. It's not mere self-expression, but formative prayer. What we might think of as extemporaneous or improvisational prayer has not been lost—it's right there in the middle in what I designate as "petition and intercession." During that time I can pray about whatever I want. But before I reach that point I first focus on being formed by a true liturgy. I never find it boring or tedious—I'm not bored with the living God who is Father, Son, and Holy Spirit. I bring my own passion to prayer. But I like arriving at the place of prayer and finding a track laid out for me. The locomotive may be full of steam but the train still needs a track. And if you stubbornly remain resistant to the idea of incorporating a formal liturgy into your prayer life, I will remind you that you already have one! You already have an established pattern of prayer. You tend to pray in the same way day after day—assuming you pray day after day. What the vetted liturgies of the church do is give us something better than a shoddy do-it-your-self liturgy. The opportunity to pour out your heart to God is still there. But now it's buttressed by Scripture, creed, and liturgy. If I arrive at the time of prayer with a worried mind or troubled emotions, I find it comforting and helpful to have ten minutes or so of prescribed liturgy before I begin to pour out my lament.

For the past several years I've taught a five-session prayer class using this liturgy. It is one of the best things I've done as a pastor. On a regular basis people tell me how the use of this liturgy has transformed their prayer life. Eventually, people outside of our church heard about the prayer school and asked if I would record it. We record all of our sermons and put them online for free. But I hesitated at recording the prayer school. Prayer seems like something that should be taught face to face, almost whispered, like telling a secret. So I've declined to record it. I've clung to the oral tradition in this one area. Then people began to request that we offer the prayer school over a weekend so they could travel to St. Joseph to be a part of it. I agreed to do this. We did no advertising other than to announce the dates, but the first time we offered the weekend version of prayer school we had people attend from seventeen states! That's a powerful testimony. Modern Christians have a deep desire to be taught how to pray well.

People who have encountered Jesus want to pray, but they don't know how. We have made the mistake of thinking people can pray well with desire and instinct alone. But it's not true. Somehow we thought telling the Christian seeker to "just talk to God" was enough. It's not enough. Telling people to pray but not teaching them *how* to pray only leads to frustration. Sadly, for these frustrated people, prayer often becomes a giant cesspool of guilt.

They've been given an intolerable burden. They've been told to pray, but they've not been given the resources to pray well. Among the most noble vocations in pastoral work is teaching people how to pray. Prayer that cannot access vintage liturgies is watered-down prayer. When prayer turns from water to wine, it's absolutely wonderful!

Chapter 5

Sitting With Jesus

I lit a candle and kneeled in prayer. I chanted a psalm, prayed the liturgy, and offered my petitions. Then I sat in a chair. Quiet and alone. But not alone. Jesus was in the room with me. I was aware of this. I acknowledged Jesus by simply being aware of his presence. I said nothing. I waited. I didn't anticipate anything. I wasn't asking for anything. I was just present to the presence of Jesus. Then I was shown something. An event from my life fifteen years earlier. An evening in 1991. It was more vivid than a memory. It was, if I can use the word, something like a vision. I saw myself watching the bombing of Baghdad on live television, eating pizza, and enjoying it. I wasn't conflicted. I wasn't grieved. I was entertained…by laser-guided bombs and the death they wrought. I watched my thirty-two-year-old self in a vision. Then, as I sat with Jesus and was confronted with this long-forgotten episode, Jesus spoke to me. Just five words. He said, "That was your worst sin." I wept bitterly. I repented deeply. That moment of sitting with Jesus, though it may sound cliché, changed me. It changed my life and ministry. I've not been the same since.

In my morning liturgy of prayer, there is a section designated by just one word—contemplation. But it's a big deal. Contemplation, or contemplative prayer, has the potential to be the most transformative practice in our life. It is the way out of the cramped prison of dualism. As long as we remain imprisoned in the reactive world of dualistic thinking, spiritual growth is impossible. There are transformations that can occur only if we learn to look at the world free from the distorting lens of us-versus-them dualism. If we always look at the world through our single-view lenses, we will never change. Contemplation offers us a new way of looking at the world. In order to see the world the way God sees it, we need some contemplative breakthroughs.

> Contemplation, or contemplative prayer, has the potential to be the most transformative practice in our life. It is the way out of the cramped prison of dualism.

In the tenth chapter of Acts, we find the fascinating story of the Apostle Peter's contemplative breakthrough—a breakthrough that altered the entire course of Christianity. The fisherman turned apostle was staying in the seaside town of Joppa. At noon he went up on the roof to observe one of the designated Jewish hours of prayer. While in prayer, the Scripture tells us Peter went into a trance (*ekstasis*) and saw something—a great sheet filled with non-kosher animals being let down from the sky. A voice instructed him to "kill and eat." Peter refused, saying, "By no means, Lord; for I have never eaten anything that is profane or unclean." The voice from heaven replied, "What God has made clean, you must not call profane." This happened three times. Because of this mystical experience, Peter was willing to accept an invitation to enter the home of a Gentile—something he had never done before. When Peter arrived at the home of Cornelius, a military officer in the occupying Roman army, Peter said:

> You yourselves know that it is unlawful for a Jew to associate with or visit a Gentile; but God has shown me that I should not call anyone profane or unclean…I truly understand that God shows no partiality, but in every nation anyone who fears him and does what is right is acceptable to him. (Acts 10:28, 34–35)

The implications of this breakthrough are incalculable. Peter's new perspective opened the door for the gospel of Messiah to be preached to Gentiles, and this changed the world. But how did Peter arrive at this new perspective? How did Peter become open to a revolutionary concept of inclusion that would challenge all the established norms of his religious worldview? The answer is contemplative prayer.

Peter had been a disciple of Jesus for three years. He was a witness of the risen Christ. And now, ten years later, he was the leading apostle of the new Christian faith. But Peter had a limited Hebrew-centric worldview. For Peter, Yahweh was the God of Jews only. Jesus was the Messiah for Jews only. The body of Messiah was for Jews only. If Gentiles wanted to be accepted by Yahweh and saved by the Messiah, they had to become Jews first. That meant being circumcised, keeping kosher, and observing Torah. Peter was locked into a Jewish-only perspective of God, Jesus, and the gospel. This was not just Peter's theological perspective, it was his personal identity. It was how he understood his place in the world. What Peter knew for sure was that to be accepted by God one had to be a Jew! Gentiles were *persona non grata*, they were not welcome at God's banqueting table.

But Peter's ethnocentric perspective began to change when he had a contemplative breakthrough while praying on Simon the Tanner's rooftop. In a trance he was shown non-kosher food and told by God to *break the law of Moses* and eat it! Peter was being instructed to transgress the Torah! Talk about cognitive dissonance! But Peter got the message—he was to stop thinking of other people as non-kosher and unacceptable to God. Now Peter would break the Jewish law he had always observed and enter the home of a Gentile! Without a contemplative breakthrough this would have been utterly impossible.

When news of Peter's radical inclusive theology and hospitality reached Jerusalem, the circumcision party was appalled! I find it interesting that only ten years into the history of Christianity there were already exclusivist factions. Their particular obsession was to make sure no one was admitted into the church who was not first circumcised and properly vetted as Jewish. Later the Apostle Paul will go toe-to-toe with the circumcision party, but Peter was the first to challenge the "Jews only" understanding of salvation. When Peter arrived in Jerusalem and was challenged by the arch-conservative circumcision party, Peter defended himself by recounting his mystical experience and the change in perspective it produced. Eventually the first church council would settle the matter in favor of including Gentiles *as Gentiles* in the community of Messiah (see Acts 15).

What Peter experienced on the rooftop in Joppa is a form of contemplative prayer. Christian mystics and monks as early as the third century have spoken of this practice. It's something I stumbled upon in my own experiments with prayer. I didn't know the term contemplative prayer. I simply thought of it as "sitting with Jesus." I had found that when I was in prayer, if I would just sit with Jesus over things that were troubling or perplexing, I would often begin to gain a new perspective. In prayer, I would acknowledge the situation or person or question or issue that I was troubled or perplexed about and sit with it in the presence of Jesus. The three of us—Jesus, "it", and I—would sit together. What tended to happen over time was that anger, fear, and prejudice would subside enough to allow for the possibility of a new perspective. I knew this was a good practice. It was producing good fruit in my life. Eventually I discovered that what I thought of as "sitting with Jesus" is what others for centuries had been calling contemplative prayer. This practice of contemplation changed me. The ideas on forgiveness and beauty and peace that would later become my books *Unconditional?, Beauty Will Save the World,* and *A Farewell To Mars* were born during these times of contemplation.

Contemplative prayer is prayer without agenda, and largely without words. But this is not to be confused with just "thinking" about something. This is bringing the issue into the presence of Jesus—the Light who coming into the world enlightens every person (John 1:4). It's during contemplative prayer that we can begin to move out of the darkness of fear-based bias into the light of Christ. It works like this—when we feel hurt, threatened, or angered by a person, people-group, opinion, or situation, we instinctively look through the lens of self-defense. It's like looking at something through the sights of a gun—it's a narrow perspective framed in fear and held in hostility. Such a perspective is certainly not the full or true perspective. But if we are dualistic, non-contemplative people, we will think of our highly limited perspective as total truth. It's all we can see. This is the black-and-white world where everything is framed as win-or-lose, us-versus-them. This was the perspective of the circumcision party when they heard the audacious claim from their preeminent apostle that Gentiles were acceptable to God *as Gentiles*. As long as they viewed the world through the lens of win-or-lose and us-versus-them, Peter's claim that Gentiles were accepted by God would be deeply unsettling.

> Prayer that reinforces our egocentric tendencies is entirely counterproductive. The formation of liturgical prayer is necessary to arrive at the place of true contemplation.

All they could see was the loss of privilege and a threat to their sense of identity. To change that kind of perspective requires a contemplative breakthrough. This is why debates between non-contemplative people are so intractable and fruitless.

Peter said that his new perspective came to him while he was in a trance or ecstasy. The Greek word is *ekstasis* and it means to stand outside of yourself. *Ekstasis* is precisely the goal of contemplative prayer—to gain a perspective that is outside our self-interested, self-defensive, egocentric perspective. As long as we look at the world through the eyes of self-interest and self-defense we will never see the world as God sees it. Contemplation can lead us to a breakthrough. But you can't rush into contemplation. You first have to arrive in the presence of Jesus. This is why you need the discipline of formative prayer before you can engage in contemplative prayer. People who try contemplation without first being properly formed in prayer just end up thinking their same old thoughts and calling them Jesus! Prayer that reinforces our egocentric tendencies is entirely counterproductive. The formation of liturgical prayer is necessary to arrive at the place of true contemplation.

But do we really want a contemplative breakthrough? We may not want to gain a 360-degree perspective. We may prefer viewing the world through our gunsights. It's simpler that way. Every conflict can be framed as good versus evil...and we always get to wear the white hat. Contemplation changes all of that...we see a whole lot more gray hats. We prefer to imagine the world as neatly divided between heroes and villains who are easily identifiable. Ambiguity irritates the reactive soul. If you gain a new perspective beyond the cherished opinions of groupthink hostility, you have to decide what to do with it. If you choose to go public with your new perspective, you may very well be subject to vicious criticism from the old guard. There's

> Prayer is not about persuading God to do our bidding, prayer is about coming to see the world through God's eyes of love.

always a circumcision party who will angrily defend their exclusivist position. Paul called them dogs and said, "Beware!" (Philippians 3:2).

The ultimate goal of contemplation is not just a new way of seeing, but love. Everything about God tends toward love. God is love. The highest form of knowing is not empiricism or rational thought—as the Enlightenment told us—but love. For the Christian, true enlightenment doesn't come from empiricism but from Christ. Christian enlightenment is not about rationalism, it's about love. You don't really know a thing until you love it. You don't really know people until you love them. But if you see a person or group primarily as a rival posing a threat to your self-interest, you cannot love them. You will only fear them, and reacting in fear you will lash out at them. A contemplative breakthrough makes love possible. This is what happened to Peter. Jesus' disciples had to learn to love Samaritans and Gentiles. Prior to Pentecost they were comfortable excluding them and at times even advocated violence against them (see Matthew 15:23 and Luke 9:54). But when Peter and the rest of the Apostles came to see the Gentiles as accepted by God, they could learn to love them. That's when Peter could preach the Gospel to Gentiles. Peter could not preach the gospel in the power of the Spirit to Cornelius until he could act according to love, until he became open to seeing and accepting Cornelius as a human being loved and accepted by God.

So why didn't the Holy Spirit give Peter his contemplative breakthrough ten years earlier? Who knows? We all have to walk the road set before us and the journey takes time. The Spirit woos us, but does not force us. The Spirit gives hints, but we must connect the dots. These things take time. It may take years of formative prayer before a contemplative breakthrough is possible. Many never reach the point where they are willing to see excluded others as accepted by God. They have too much fear; too much of their identity is invested in a dualistic us-versus-them perspective. Excluding those they view through the gunsights of hostility is the organizing principle of their lives. It tells them who to love and who to hate, who to embrace and who to fight. Through a contemplative breakthrough the Apostle Peter got beyond his us-versus-them dualism and was able to see that the kosher and non-kosher division of humanity was a fear-based construct no longer authorized by God. Peter's breakthrough changed the world. Over the next few centuries, the Gentile world of the Roman Empire would be converted to Christ. It began with Peter's contemplative breakthrough on the rooftop of a tanner.

Your own contemplative breakthrough may not change the course of world history, but it will change the course of your life! Contemplation is the way out of the cage of fear and anger. But remember, you don't begin with contemplation, you begin with liturgy. Until you are properly formed in prayer, you're not ready for a contemplative breakthrough. As long as you are in charge of your own praying, you will never see the world significantly different than you do now. Prayer is not about persuading God to do our bidding, prayer is about coming to see the world through God's eyes of love. You can get there faster if you say (and mean), "Lord, I'm willing to see this differently. I'm willing and I want to see this through your eyes." It is the world of God's eternal love that opens to us as we learn to sit with Jesus.

> "God loved us before he made us; and his love has
> never diminished and never shall."
> –Julian of Norwich[1]

Sometime after I had begun the practice of sitting with Jesus I had another dream. I dreamed I was sitting in a waiting room. I was there to meet Jesus. A few others were in the waiting room with me. In my dream I knew Jesus was on the other side of the door at the far end of the waiting room. I was terribly nervous. My hands were sweating. I was trying to prepare what I would say. As strange as it may sound, I was very concerned to not appear foolish before Jesus, so I was trying to come up with something intelligent to say. Finally my name was called and I was escorted to the door and told to enter the room. It was a white room—white walls, ceiling, and floor. Sitting in a simple white chair was Jesus. There was a second white chair sitting in front of Jesus. I knew I was to sit in that chair. But the moment I saw Jesus I lost all my composure, forgot everything I had prepared to say, and fell at his feet crying uncontrollably. I felt very foolish. Finally Jesus spoke, "Brian, what do you want?" My mind was racing. I seemed to know that whatever I requested would be granted. What *did* I want? Success? Influence? Knowledge? Revelation? Growth? These things went through my mind. But they were not what I wanted. Finally I said, "Jesus, I want to be a part of what you are doing." Jesus touched me. And I woke up. My pillow was wet with tears. Today I dare to hope that Jesus is in the process of granting my request.

Chapter 6

Echoes, Silence, Patience & Grace

I was riding the train from Rome to Assisi and it was one of the best days of my life. But the story starts back in 1993 when I preached a sermon entitled *"What To Do On the Worst Day of Your Life."* It's a sermon from 1 Samuel 30 where David loses everything to marauding raiders but recovers it all through faith in God. I used it as a kind of template for how to respond to hard times with prayer and trust. It was just a sermon, but it turned out to be a popular sermon. This was in the days of cassette tapes. Eventually, "bootlegged" copies of "What To Do On the Worst Day of Your Life" were in circulation. Over time I began to receive letters from people telling me how this sermon had helped them make it through a difficult period in their life. Some of those letters came from as far away as Africa, India, and the Philippines. Friends urged me to turn the sermon into a book. So in March of 1997 I checked into a hotel and wrote a 140-page book in three days. (That still amazes me!) With a loaf of bread and a package of salami sitting next to the desktop computer I'd hauled into the hotel room, I began to write. Three days later I had a book. I gave it the over-the-top title of the sermon—*What To Do On the Worst Day of Your Life*. I self-published it, sold five thousand copies, and forgot about it.

Fifteen years later in December of 2008, as the world reeled from a global financial crisis, a publisher contacted me wanting to do a major hardback release of *What To Do On the Worst Day of Your Life*. I hadn't thought of it for years. The publisher felt it offered hope to people who were afraid of the future and suffering loss in the financial crisis. They wanted to publish it immediately. At first I was flattered, but when I reread what I had written eleven years earlier, I cringed with embarrassment. It was poorly written. (What do you expect from a book written in three days?) But worse, it was far too prescriptive and promised way too much. It was an example of faith presented as formulaic certitude—the kind of distorted faux-faith I had turned away from. It came across as, "follow these ten steps and—*voila!* —all your problems will be solved." Worst of all, some of my theological assertions were just plain wrong. Self-published words from my first-half-of-life self were coming back to haunt me. So I told the publisher I wasn't interested. This led to a strange conversation over several days where a publisher was insisting that a book was great and was offering money to bring it out in hardback, while the author was insisting that it was lousy and would best be forgotten. This doesn't happen very often. Eventually I suggested that perhaps I could rewrite it. The agreement was that I would rewrite the book in three weeks—the book I had written eleven years earlier in three days. The publisher's main request was that I not change very much. I ended up rewriting almost every sentence. I kept the same ten chapter titles, but in the end it was a very different book. I signed the contract two days before Christmas. I delivered the rewritten manuscript on January 8. *What To Do On the Worst Day of Your Life* was released on February 17, 2009. (That too still amazes me!)

It was a crazy three weeks. I was trying to rewrite a book that obviously offered real hope to people, but one that also had serious flaws. I was trying to blend old and new in a faithful way. I was attempting to be like the kingdom-minded scribe Jesus talked about when he said, "Every scribe who has been trained for the kingdom of heaven is like the master of a household who brings out of his treasure what is new and what is old" (Matthew 13:52). And I was doing all this during the Christmas holidays...and while on an international trip! The final week of rewriting was done while Peri and I were in Rome. We were staying in a romantic little hotel a few blocks from the Coliseum. We would tour Rome during the day and I would write at night. It was a hectic time, but it's a fond memory. I still remember sitting by the fireplace in the lobby of our hotel on a cold rainy night in Rome and finishing the project by writing a new preface. In part I wrote:

> Recently while in Rome I walked on the *Via Triumphalis*—the ancient road of the Roman victory parade. Victorious emperors and generals led their armies in a celebration of triumph. The apostle Paul was aware of the Roman victory

parade and used it as a metaphor describing our life in Christ. In his letter to the Colossian church, the great apostle tells us that we are always being led in the victory parade of Christ. … But it doesn't always seem like it. It doesn't always feel like we are living life in a victory parade. Sometimes life feels more like a death march than a ticker-tape parade. Fortunately, the Bible doesn't ignore this experience or shy away from addressing such realities. The Scriptures don't flinch from telling the stories of hardship and tragedy visited upon the righteous. The overarching storyline of the Bible is *not*, "Once upon a time, they lived happily ever after." Instead, the divine story of God's people has plenty of moments where the narrative, in effect, says, "Then all hell broke loose." The glorious thing about the chronicles of Scripture is that disappointment is never the end of the story—not for those who believe God. Instead, the barren do give birth, the slaves *are* set free, the promised land *is* found, the temple *is* built…and rebuilt, Messiah d*oes* appear, the kingdom *does* come, and the dead *are* raised. And in the story we have before us now, David does recover from the worst day of his life. This is why people have loved the Bible for thousands of years—people of every age need hope.[1]

Meeting the deadline for the rewrite was a relief. A book that belonged to another lifetime was now a book my post-2004 self could feel good about...even if the title was still a bit cheesy. I sent the finished manuscript for *What To Do On the Worst Day of Your Life* to the publisher. The next day was one of the best days of my life. If I could pick one day to live over and over, like Bill Murray in *Groundhog Day*, it might be this day. It was the day Peri and I took the train from Rome to Assisi. We would spend two nights in Assisi before returning to Rome. I wanted to go to this medieval hilltop town in Umbria because I had become fascinated with Francis—the famous thirteenth-century saint of Assisi.

Two years earlier I had been meeting with a group of young men who felt called to the ministry. One evening a week we would gather in my basement for two hours; we prayed together and discussed Jesus and theology. I jokingly called it the school of Tyrannus—the lecture hall where Paul taught his disciples in Ephesus

About the time my fascination with the frontier revivalists had begun to wane, my fascination with Saint Francis was born. My tolerance for *Grapes of Wrath* revivalism had worn thin.

(Acts 19:9). I affectionately referred to the young men as my little dinosaurs for Jesus. At the end of our "school of Tyrannus" my students gave me a book as a gift. In the front of it they wrote, "Thanks for creating new dinosaurs!" The book was *Francis of Assisi: A Revolutionary Life* by Adrian House. It was my introduction to Saint Francis—at least an introduction to a Francis beyond garden statues and the hippie troubadour of the 1970s film *Brother Sun, Sister Moon*.

Adrian House's scholarly biography introduced me to a more

historical and more revolutionary Francis. I was captivated. Over the next two years I read a dozen more biographies on Francis. The saint of Assisi was becoming my new hero. And I needed some new heroes. About the time my fascination with the frontier revivalists had begun to wane, my fascination with Saint Francis was born. My tolerance for *Grapes of Wrath* revivalism had worn thin. The histrionics of Billy Sunday style evangelism now left a sour taste in my mouth. I had cut my teeth on the eighteenth and nineteenth-century revivalists, but after three decades of that kind of Christianity, I came to realize that contemporary revivalism fails to engage the wider culture in any meaningful way and in the end it just wears people out. What is called "revival" today is mostly spectacle and religious entertainment playing upon the emotions of guilt, desire, and anger. I was more interested in a quieter and, ultimately more revolutionary, approach to living the Christian life. The gentle Francis offered me a better model than the raging revivalist.

Francis was born into the home of a well-to-do merchant. As a youth he regaled Assisi with his exuberant mirth and extravagant parties. For a time he tried his hand at being a knight. But after the bloody horrors of battle and being held as a prisoner of war for a year, Francis lost his taste for martial glory. In 1204 a twenty-three-year-old Francis, despondent and facing a crisis about what to do with his life, was praying in an abandoned chapel on the outskirts of Assisi. While gazing upon a Byzantine crucifix a voice from the cross said, "Francis, go and rebuild my church, which you see is falling into ruin." Taking the instructions literally, Francis set about repairing the broken-down San Damiano chapel. Eventually Francis, with the blessing of Pope Innocent III, came to understand that his calling was not to refurbish dilapidated chapels, but to restore a compromised church. With eleven other brothers the Franciscan order was born. Within twenty years, forty thousand people had joined this radical countercultural movement! It is one of the most remarkable moments in church history. Francis lived his extraordinary life as a kind of sacred performance art demonstrating an alternative to the materialism and militarism that characterized thirteenth-century Italy. In an age of pride, avarice, and violence, Francis modeled humility, simplicity, and gentleness, and gained a new hearing for the gospel. It's not hard to understand why the life of Saint Francis can be viewed as a prophetic witness to our own age.

If you are interested in learning more about the life of Saint Francis, there is no lack of resources. It's been said that more books have been written on the life of Francis of Assisi than any other historical figure other than Jesus Christ. Of the Francis books I've read, my favorite may be G.K. Chesterton's slim volume, *Saint Francis of Assisi*. In this charming tome, Chesterton audaciously calls Francis "the only Christian"—meaning that if anyone since the Apostles has ever come close enough to imitating Jesus to be worthy of the moniker "Christlike," it was Francis. At the end of his meditation on Francis, Chesterton says, "It is perhaps the chief suggestion of this book that Saint Francis walked the world like the Pardon of God."[2] I like that. Francis didn't spend much time railing against the predominant sins of his age—egregious as they were; instead he offered sinners the pardon of God and modeled a different way to live. Like I said, it's easy to see why Francis can be viewed as a prophetic witness to our own age.

So after the rewrite of *Worst Day* was over, Peri and I spent a couple of wonderful days in Assisi. We hired a local guide and

Francis scholar to help us explore the world of Saint Francis, Saint Clare, and the early Franciscans—those revolutionary thirteenth-century Christians whose radical lifestyles brought spiritual renewal to a moribund church and turned medieval Christendom upside down. Our two days in Assisi were beautiful and spiritually invigorating. I was deeply moved when I saw the San Damiano crucifix from which Francis heard the voice of Jesus call him to rebuild his church. Three years later we made a second pilgrimage to Assisi trying to imbibe more of the revolutionary spirit of Saint Francis.

> I needed to hear echoes from the past. I needed to practice more silence in the present. I needed patience with the future. I needed grace to tie it all together.

Ian Cron wrote a lovely novel about an American evangelical megachurch pastor who travels to Assisi in search of a richer faith. I didn't read *Chasing Francis* until after my two trips to Assisi, but when I met Ian Cron I thanked him for writing a novel about me! (Sort of.)

On that January morning in 2009 as we rode the train from Rome to Assisi I was listening to the Foo Fighters' album *Echoes, Silence, Patience & Grace*. At the same time I was researching the great creeds of Christianity—the Apostles' Creed, the Nicene Creed, the Athanasian Creed—on my iPhone. It was a synchronicity of centuries—second-century creed and confession, twenty-first-century music and technology, while on my way to explore the haunts of a thirteenth-century saint. At some point I noticed what I was doing. I had to smile. I wasn't trying to return to an earlier time, but I was trying to pull the past into the present. I wasn't a naive idealist trying to recreate a romantic past. I simply wanted to access forgotten treasures of the past to enrich the present. I couldn't return to the days of the Nicene Fathers or Francis of Assisi (and I had no desire to do so). But I could explore their contributions while being fully engaged with my own era. I also thought about the name of the album I was listening to—*Echoes, Silence, Patience & Grace*. Those four words seemed prescient. I don't want to make too much of what was probably just a happy coincidence, but those four words did speak to me. Echoes, silence, patience, and grace. These were things I needed. I needed to hear echoes from the past. I needed to practice more silence in the present. I needed patience with the future. I needed grace to tie it all together. Like the five words in 2004, these four words in 2009 meant something to me. Four words from the Foo Fighters on the train to Assisi. Well, if God can speak to Balaam through a donkey, why can't God speak to me through a rock band?

ECHOES

My favorite place in Paris is Notre Dame Cathedral. I've been there a lot. I'm drawn to this marvel of gothic architecture. I like the soaring arches and the flying buttresses. I like the feel of the worn-smooth stone floor and the beauty of timeless stained glass. I even have an affection for the gargoyles that peer down impassively upon the unsuspecting tourists. I like Notre Dame mostly because it's old and so much different from the spaces of worship I've known in America. When I visit a twelfth-century gothic cathedral, I feel a tangible connection with Christian faith from a distant past—I feel it in the very stones. If I find myself there during a vesper service I hear the echoes of ancient faith in the haunting beauty of Gregorian chants.

Echoes are the return of earlier sounds. I needed to hear the distant echoes of an earlier Christianity. That's why I was on the train to Assisi. I was beginning to understand how important it is to maintain an ongoing conversation with the Christians who have lived before us. We must resist the tyranny of the present. If we ignore the echoes of the past, we doom ourselves to an unrecognized ignorance. It's only because of our connection with our technological past that we don't have to reinvent the wheel every generation. Likewise, if we maintain a connection with our theological past, we don't have to reformulate the essential creeds every generation. When I encounter people attempting to reformulate the nature of the Trinity, I think, *don't you know we settled this in 325*? Of course, they may very well *not* know! Or if they do know, they don't care. They have no respect for the past. To them it's just *old*—and old means obsolete, which is, of course, a ridiculous notion peculiar to the modern era.

> The Holy Spirit has never abandoned the church. Every generation had those who heard and spoke what the Spirit said to the church.

One of the problems with revivalism is its egocentric obsession with the present and its woeful ignorance of the past. I'm acquainted with two large and popular charismatic ministries who have identified themselves in the Book of Revelation. For real. They've hijacked the great vision of John the Revelator, making it not only about the early twenty-first century, but about them! With no long view of church history and no broad view of the church's global work, everything has to be right now and right here. So while one ministry claims a connection to the two witnesses in Revelation 11, another ministry identifies themselves as the first angel in Revelation 14. It's all a bit much.

For too much of my life, my idea of church history went something like this—the church started off great with Pentecost, jumped the tracks a couple of centuries later, got back on track with the Reformation, and really took off with Azusa Street. The arrogance is appalling. It's why most modern revivalist movements seem to follow this implicit dictum: Refound the church and prepare for Armageddon. Contemporary revivalist movements always seem convinced that they're the first generation to recover "apostolic purity" and the last generation before the return of the Lord. They misappropriate 1 Peter 2:9 as they brashly claim, "We are the chosen generation." Without a clear memory of church history we become the Alpha and Omega in our imagined self-importance. Christian amnesiacs could benefit from some echoes—the echoes of Athanasius and Aquinas, Irenaeus and Erasmus, Clement and the Cappadocian Fathers. The Holy Spirit has never abandoned the church. Every generation had those who heard and spoke what the Spirit said to the church. We should pay attention to their echoes.

I hear the echoes of my earlier sisters and brothers as I muse upon their time-tested wisdom. In an age of pragmatism where the mystics are muted, the echoes of the ancient Christian mystics are good for my soul—mystics like Julian of Norwich and John of the Cross. John talks to me about the dark night of the soul, while Julian shares her revelations of divine love. They tell me secrets—secrets I may never have discovered on my own. John says, "It is love alone that unites the soul with God,"[3] while Julian whispers, "All will be well, and all will be well, and all manner of things will be well."[4] I need those echoes.

I can discern the holy echoes of another time when I visit the great cathedrals and basilicas of the old world. It's true that I often feel conflicted in these gilded sanctuaries. More than once I've sat in St. Peter's Basilica in Rome wondering, *is this a good thing?* The question is a valid one and does not yield a simple answer. But there is no mistaking that there was a time when architecture itself was an act of worship—something that is sadly foreign to most American evangelicals. Living in a nation dotted with utilitarian, nondescript, multi-use church buildings, I can celebrate the desire to create sacred space through sacred architecture. I'm glad we have these sacred echoes in our increasingly secular world. When I have the opportunity to visit one of these churches, I try to do so, not as a tourist, but as a worshiper. When I take time to pray beneath those vaulted ceilings with their soaring arches and stained glass windows, I can sense the echoes from worshipers of long ago. I can share the awe that filled their souls. The believers who built those cathedrals, who were baptized and received communion there, who prayed and worshiped there, are my brothers and sisters. I esteem their way of worship— even if they didn't have a rock band, a light show, and a fog machine.

By listening to the echoes of an older Christianity, we gain a better sense of our own place in the long history of the church. We are not chained to the past, we are free to innovate. We must constantly translate Christianity into contemporary culture, but we do so by maintaining a conversation with our mothers and fathers, with our older sisters and brothers. Their echoes are important, their voices need to be respected. Christianity doesn't belong exclusively to the living, but is the shared faith of all who have confessed Christ. This is why tradition matters. G.K. Chesterton called it "the democracy of the dead":

> Tradition means giving a vote to the most obscure of all classes, our ancestors. It is the democracy of the dead. Tradition refuses to submit to the small and arrogant oligarchy of those who merely happen to be walking about.[5]

SILENCE

Ours is an angry and vociferous age. We're constantly subjected to the noise of charged political rhetoric—the wearying din of the culture wars. Too often Sunday morning can be little more than a religious echo of this same noise. But shouldn't Sunday be a Christian Sabbath, a time to quiet our souls and receive the gift of silence? What if, instead of being another contributor to this clatter, our churches became a shelter from the storm offering respite to shell-shocked souls?

When birdsong and gentle footfall replace the shrill rancor of 24-7 news and the inane blare from five-hundred channels, the soul has a chance to heal.

Echoes and silence. Echo is the return of an earlier sound. Silence belongs to an earlier age. Ours is an age of noise. With our technological progress has come the din of modernity. With the advent of digital social media has come the white noise of everyone "expressing themselves." Silence is now a precious commodity, a scarce resource hard to come by. Sure, we can pray anywhere, anytime, but to pray well, to pray in a way that restores the soul, we need to find some quiet places. This is what we find appealing in the holy hush of the cathedral, the sacred stillness of the monastery, the reverent quiet of the woods. When birdsong and gentle footfall replace the shrill rancor of 24-7 news and the inane blare from five-hundred channels, the soul has a chance to heal. Without some intentional silence the weary soul is a prisoner being slowly worked to death in a merciless gulag of endless noise. The always-posted sign at the entrance of the tourist-attracting cathedrals is perhaps a desperate plea from the soul of modern man—Silence, Please.

It's not just the silence of prayer that is needed—a posture of quietude needs to be adopted by contemporary Christianity, especially in North America. Too much of the most visible presence of Christianity is loud, vociferous, and angry. It bears a closer resemblance to shock-jocks than Saint Francis. And I don't hesitate to suggest that Francis of Assisi might offer us a better model than Rush of Limbaugh. We don't need to add more noise to the raging tumult that is America. We have enough of that as it is…and it's not helping. Thirteenth-century Italy had plenty of social and political problems, but Francis found a more creative way to respond than by yelling at people. His own life of prayer, peace, and poverty offered a quiet critique of systemic sin, while demonstrating the alternative way of Christ. In our discordant times we need our churches to be more like Saint Francis and less like Fox News. We need a quieter, less combative, less belligerent Christianity. More quietness and trust, less riot and protest.

As Isaiah dreamed of the coming reign of God, he expressed his hope in a line of poetry by saying, "The effect of righteousness will be peace, and the result of righteousness, quietness and trust" (Isaiah 32:17). Isaiah sees the result of the reign of God as quietness and trust, not riot and protest. There are those who are fascinated by a kind of "riot Christianity" where the point is to make a lot of noise. They try to make a case for it by saying things like, "Everywhere Paul went there were riots." Well, perhaps. But the riots weren't Paul's doing or desire. In Jerusalem, Paul was arrested after being *falsely* accused of starting a riot. In arguing his innocence Paul says, "They did not find me disputing with anyone or stirring up a crowd" (Acts 24:21). Paul never advocates for angry, loud, public protest, but just the opposite. Paul says we should "aspire to live quietly" (1 Thessalonians 4:11) and "lead a quiet and peaceable life" (1 Timothy 2:2). Paul doesn't advocate riot Christianity, but quiet Christianity. Riots are the work of the devil, not the Holy Spirit.

A paradigm of protest and a preoccupation with power has given us wrong ideas. When we imagine the kingdom of God coming as a tsunami of irresistible force, we think our public presence needs to be loud, demonstrative, and even combative. This is entirely wrong. Babylon is built by the noisy machinery of war, conquest, and power politics, but not the kingdom of God. Almost all of Jesus' kingdom parables are quiet stories. According to Jesus the kingdom of God is like seed being sown, like plants growing, like bread rising. It's domestic, not militant. It's like a woman sweeping her house, like a shepherd searching for a lost sheep, like a wayward son coming home at last. It never gets much louder than the music and dancing of a house party. This is a long way from a riot.

Because we are obsessed with all things "big" and "powerful" in the conventional sense, we are convinced that to change the world the kingdom of God needs to sound like a deafening construction site—bulldozers and jackhammers. But the kingdom coming isn't as much like a construction site as a forest growing. Even if we do think of the kingdom as the construction of a holy temple, we're reminded that too much noise is incompatible with the sacred. There was this unique protocol in Solomon's construction of the temple, "In building the temple, only blocks dressed at the quarry were used, and no hammer, chisel or any other iron tool was heard at the temple site while it was being built" (1 Kings 6:7, NIV).

During his ministry Jesus refused to contribute to the combative noise of his age—even when his opponents were aching for a fight.

> When Jesus became aware of this, he departed. Many crowds followed him, and he cured all of them, and ordered them not to make him known. This was to fulfill what had been spoken through the prophet Isaiah:
>
>> "Here is my servant, whom I have chosen,
>> my beloved, with whom my soul is well pleased.
>> I will put my Spirit upon him,
>> and he will proclaim justice to the Gentiles.
>> He will not wrangle or cry aloud,
>> Nor will anyone hear his voice in the streets."
>> (Matthew 12:15–19)

The church is not a special interest group that has to make its demands known. We don't have to "fight for our rights" anymore than Jesus did. We don't have to mimic the noise of special-interest anger. We can be an alternative of quietness and trust. The church doesn't have to make things happen, it can simply be that part of the world that trusts God and lives under the peaceable reign of Christ here and now. As Yves Congar has said, "The Church is not a special little group, isolated, apart...The Church is the world as believing in Christ."[6] In a world that surely must grow weary of the harsh blare of ideological anger, the church is to be a haven of quietness and trust, a gentle refuge of peace.

PATIENCE

The first Sunday in November, 2006, we celebrated the twenty-fifth anniversary of Word of Life Church. Following the services Peri and I flew to Tel Aviv and from there to Eilat on the Red Sea. The next morning, with luggage in tow, we walked across the border to Egypt where we were met by Mina—a Coptic Christian guide, Akhmed—a Bedouin driver, and Mohammad—an Egyptian security guard from Cairo. We were on our way to climb Mount Sinai. I had made an appointment to meet God on the summit of Sinai at sunrise on November 9, 2006. This was the thirty-second anniversary of my teenage encounter with Jesus and, as I thought of it, the beginning of the second half of my ministry. I wanted to re-consecrate my life and ministry on the mountain where Moses met with God.

Introductions were made, the five of us piled into a Toyota Land Cruiser, and we headed into the desert...off road. Only a Bedouin driver familiar with the Sinai wilderness could have pulled this off. It was an unbelievably rough ride and I was terribly carsick. After stopping along the way to explore the Colored

Canyon and have a meal at a Bedouin camp, we reached our lodging around 10:00 p.m. We were up at 2:00 a.m. to climb the mountain. It was a short night. We were told it would take us about four hours to reach the summit, but we made it in two. So for another two hours we shivered in the dark in freezing temperatures awaiting sunrise. But the cold, dark wait was worth it. It was the most memorable sunrise of my life. We kept our appointment with God and then began our descent. By mid-morning we arrived at St. Catherine's Monastery at the foot of the holy mountain. This monastery dating back to the fourth century is the oldest site of continuous Christian worship in the world. Orthodox monks have been praying here day and night for seventeen centuries. I wanted to join them in prayer. At first the monks refused since we were not Orthodox, but with a bit of pleading and cajoling they allowed us into the chapel where we added our voices to seventeen centuries of prayer.

In my visits to Assisi, Notre Dame, the Church of the Holy Sepulchre, and St. Catherine's Monastery I'm reminded of the antiquity of Christianity. This reminds me that I can afford to be patient. The church has been going about its work of making disciples for nearly two thousand years…and for all we know we are still the early church! (If the suggestion that we might still be the early church irritates you, could it be that I have struck a nerve of impatience?) During the Jesus Movement of the 1970s, we were all convinced that Jesus would return within a decade, two at most. We couldn't imagine a twenty-first century dawning prior to the second coming of Christ. Looking back on those days I realize that our eschatology wasn't based in any sound reading of Scripture, but in childish impatience. Everything had to happen in our lifetime.

We could not be content to be faithful in our generation and hand the task over to the next generation. No, we had to be the "omega generation." We were impatient. Of course, impatience is a hallmark of immaturity. It's the droning query from children in the backseat—"Are we there yet?"

To live a peaceable life, patience is needed. Impatience instills a permanent agitation in the soul, an agitation that makes peace impossible. Prayer is the slow process by which patience replaces agitation. Learning to pray well has acquainted me with patience. Praying the ancient psalms and the centuries old prayers of the church cultivates an appreciation for patience. I've come to realize that the main purpose of prayer is not to change the world, but to change me...and I am under the assumption that this will take a lifetime. I might naively think the world can be changed in a decade or two, but I know good and well it will take the better part of a lifetime to change me. So in prayer I learn to be patient, even with myself. Isaiah imagined the people of God as oaks of righteousness (see Isaiah 61:3). We grow like oak trees, not dandelions. Spiritual formation happens over a lifetime, not overnight. In a brilliant act of theft, Eugene Peterson lifted a phrase from Friedrich Nietzsche when he described Christian discipleship as "a long obedience in the same direction."[7] That's as good a definition of patience as any—a long obedience in the same direction. Those looking for instant results instead of a long obedience will find the Christian life disappointing.

Patience is the heart of wisdom. Impatience is the essence of foolishness. Stanley Hauerwas has correctly observed that "war is impatience."[8] When we are impatient—whining from the backseat, "Are we there yet?"—we inevitably become frustrated and quarrelsome. When we demand "results" on our own timetable,

we will most likely find ourselves out of step with the patient pace
of historic Christianity. Impatient saints don't exist. The saints have
learned the secret of being patient with the world, with themselves,
and even with God. The kingdom of Christ has more in common
with an Italian three-hour lunch than with an American drive-
though window. We may be in a hurry, but it seems God never is.
Coming to terms with the "slowness" of God is what we mean by
patience. In my youth I regarded my own impatience as a kind of
virtue, now I see it as folly, a cousin to selfishness. Today I'm trying
to learn how to mature like a dusty bottle of wine patiently resting
in God's cellar. If nothing particularly notable happens in church
history during my lifetime, I'm fine with that. It's not my church.
It's not my world. It's God's church and God's world, and God has
time on his side. I can afford to be patient.

GRACE

My father died in 2009. He was one of the wisest and kindest men
I've ever known. L. Glen Zahnd was a judge and at his funeral a
man he had once sent to prison for armed robbery came up to me
and said, "I'm here today to honor your father. In his capacity as
judge he sent me to prison, but he always treated me with respect
and kindness. He was as merciful as he could be and he strove to
preserve my dignity." My father was like that—he was a man full of
grace. He spent his last few months in a Franciscan nursing home
called La Verna. It's named after the place where St. Francis of
Assisi received the wounds of Christ. In his final years my father
suffered from dementia and could barely communicate. But
whenever he was asked if he would like to receive Communion, he

always managed to say yes. Even as his mind and body were failing him, this man known throughout the community for his kindness wanted to maintain his connection to grace.

G.K. Chesterton suggested that Saint Francis walked the world like the pardon of God. It's an apt summary of the saint's life. Francis embodied the grace of God as he walked the hills of Umbria barefoot in his patched brown habit and simple rope belt, preaching to birds and bishops. His life was a kind of performance art protest against the pervasive sins of thirteenth-century Italy—pride, avarice, corruption, and violence. Yet sinners themselves were drawn to Francis. How else do we explain why, in his lifetime, forty thousand people joined his rigorous order of radical Christianity emphasizing poverty, simplicity and humility? Like Jesus, Francis could uncompromisingly denounce systemic sin, while extending genuine compassion to the people caught in its pernicious web. To be a prophetic witness against systems of sin and a preacher of God's pardon for sinners *at the same time* is the peculiar grace at which Francis excelled and to which the church is called.

Two years before his death Francis retreated to the secluded hermitage at La Verna in the mountains of Tuscany for a protracted season of prayer. While there he experienced a mystical vision that resulted in his *stigmata*—the reproduction of the wounds of Christ in his own body. Francis bore these painful wounds until his death in 1226. Admittedly, this is a mysterious phenomenon, but I am willing to view it as Francis' final dramatic testament to how the church is to be present in the world. Along with being a prophetic witness against the principalities and powers and bearing joyful witness to the pardon of God, the church is called to participate in the sufferings of Christ. The only Christian theodicy which I find credible is the confession that God does not exempt himself from the horror of human suffering, but is fully baptized into it. God in Christ joins us in a solidarity of suffering, and somehow by his wounds we are healed. Christ saves us from sin and death only by hurling himself into the abyss. The ultimate imitation of Christ is to patiently absorb sin and offer pardon in the name of love. This is grace.

If I were to pick a single moment that most clearly demonstrates who Jesus is and how he reveals the nature of God to us, it would be the moment of crucifixion when Jesus prays, "Father, forgive them; for they do not know what they are doing" (Luke 23:34). This is grace demonstrated as a love supreme. It's an unprecedented act—a plea for the pardon of his murderers. But, perhaps even more significantly, the pardon is offered with a contemplative

> When grace is pierced, it bleeds pardon. When grace is crucified, it doesn't condemn. Crucified grace is even cognizant of how nearly impossible it is for sinful persecutors to act otherwise.

recognition that his persecutors are themselves enslaved in systems of sin that prevent them from having any real understanding of their crime or how to find their way out of it. This is the amazing grace of God that came to full expression in the life of Jesus. When grace is pierced, it bleeds pardon. When grace is crucified, it doesn't condemn. Crucified grace is even cognizant of how nearly impossible it is for sinful persecutors to act otherwise. Those who seek to imitate this kind of grace will eventually be wounded themselves—they will endure a stigmata upon their soul. They will help complete what is lacking in the afflictions of Christ (see Colossians 1:24). This is what it means to be Christlike in the fullest sense. Before we are the church triumphant, we are the church stigmatized, and we are to bear our stigma with grace.

> As it is written:
> "For your sake we are killed all day long;
> We are accounted as sheep for the slaughter."
> Yet in all these things we are more than conquerors through him who loved us.
> (Romans 8:36–37, NKJV)

We are "more than conquerors," not by winning the petty games of the rat race and wearing the tin badge of "success," but by imitating the slaughtered Lamb who sits at the right hand of God. We lessen the sin of the world by joining the Lamb of God in bearing sin and pardoning sinners. But as the church has become a powerful institution, a consort with kings and queens, a confidante of presidents and prime ministers, our dispensing of grace has become distorted. We show grace to the institutions of systemic sin while condemning the individual sinner. It should be the other way around. It was never the "rank and file" sinners who gnashed their teeth at Jesus, but those for whom the present arrangement of systemic sin was advantageous. Jesus condemned the systemic sin that preserved the status quo for the Herodians and Sadducees, but showed compassion to publicans and prostitutes. This is grace. But the church, courting the favor of the powerful, has forgotten this kind of grace. We coddle the mighty whose ire we fear and condemn the sin of the weak who pose no threat. We enthusiastically endorse the systems of greed that run Wall Street while condemning personal greed in the life of the individual working for the minimum wage. We will gladly preach a sermon against the sin of personal greed, but we dare not offer a prophetic critique of the golden calf of unfettered capitalism. Jesus and Saint Francis and Dorothy Day did the opposite. They shamed the principalities and powers, but offered pardon to the people. This is the grace of God the church is to embody.

Echoes, silence, patience, and grace on the train from Rome to Assisi. It was more than a train journey between two Italian cities —it was a metaphor for the journey I had begun. A journey that was transporting me from a status quo kind of Christianity to a more revolutionary kind of Christianity. I need to be on that journey. Maybe you do too. As for me, I hope to ride that train for the rest of my life.

Chapter 7

Grain and Grape

I did a lot of things wrong on September 11, 2001. I reacted too much and prayed too little. I led a war prayer at a citywide prayer gathering. I didn't know how to pray with the vocabulary of peace, mercy, and forgiveness. I fanned the flames of anger and beat the drums of war. I didn't know the things that make for peace. I was a Christian, but not yet a disciple of the Prince of Peace. Like I said, I did a lot of things wrong on that awful day. But the day after September 11, I did something right—I served the body and blood of Jesus to bewildered believers.

We can probably think of September 11, 2001 as the real beginning of the twenty-first century. The late twentieth-century hope that the end of the Cold War would usher in a new century of peace and prosperity collapsed with the Twin Towers. In his bullhorn moment atop the rubble of the World Trade Center, President Bush channeled the American impulse to frame what was unprecedented in the familiar terms of war. It led to the institution of endless war. (What else can a "war on terror" be but endless?) In a previous book I've told the story of my own initial complicity in the evangelical inclination to hallow American militarism and march in step with the drums of war.[1] It's something I now deeply regret. But I did respond to the events of September 11 in at least one redemptive way. The day after 9/11 we held a noon prayer meeting and we've done so every Wednesday since then. For the past fourteen years we've had a Wednesday noon prayer gathering.

The most significant thing about this is that from its inception we have served Communion. I'm not sure what instinct compelled me to offer Communion the day after 9/11, but it was right to do so and it led to important changes. Until that day we served Communion only three or four times a year.

> But the day after September 11, I did something right—I served the body and blood of Jesus to bewildered believers.

Today we may serve Communion two or three times a week. The noon prayer meeting begun the day after 9/11 was my unwitting entrance into the fathomless mystery of the Eucharist.

In preparation for the weekly noon prayer and Communion service I would put together a few remarks about the Lord's Table. Brief meditations. I assumed that after a short time I would exhaust what can be said about Communion and that I would eventually fall into a kind of routine—a repetition of the same ideas. But to my amazement this didn't happen. Instead, every time I meditated on Communion, even briefly, I saw something new. It was like a kaleidoscope of revelation; at every turn I was presented with a new pattern. It was like the widow of Zarephath's barrel of flour that was never empty and the jar of oil that never ran dry. Communion turned out to be an artesian well of endless mystery. The weekly noon prayer service became my laboratory for exploring these eucharistic mysteries. What had been a watery view of Communion was turning into wine—sacramental wine. Life is full of strange segues. A providential instinct to serve Communion the day after 9/11 put me on the path to becoming a sacramental Christian. Who could have guessed?

To be sacramental is the opposite of being secular. One way of understanding secularism is that it is the argument that nothing in the world is *ontologically* sacred—that nothing is sacred *in itself*. To the secular mind the sacred is, at most, a conferred idea, a symbolic gesture, not a genuine reality. For the secularist the sacred is mere symbol. But to this idea the Christian doctrine of the Incarnation offers a resounding, "No!" If we believe that "the Word became flesh and lived among us," (John 1:14) then

> The most effective way to resist the debilitating effects of secularism is to take the sacraments seriously.

we believe in a sacred ontology, a sacredness of being. If we hold to an orthodox doctrine of the Incarnation, we believe the flesh and blood of Jesus were divine, the flesh and blood of God. The more deeply we are influenced by the sacred mystery of the Incarnation—that God became human—the more seriously we will take the sacraments of Baptism and Communion. In a secular age the Enlightenment-influenced church desperately needs to recover the sacred through a return to sacrament. The most effective way to resist the debilitating effects of secularism is to take the sacraments seriously. The modern impulse to reduce sacrament to mere symbol is an unwitting surrender to the secular argument that nothing is truly sacred. But the body of Christ is sacred. The corporal body of the risen Jesus, the ecclesial body of the church, and the eucharistic body of Communion are all sacred. We find a sacred ontology in Paul's magisterial confession regarding the mystery of Communion:

> The cup of blessing that we bless, is it not a sharing in the blood of Christ? The bread that we break, is it not a sharing in the body of Christ? (1 Corinthians 10:16)

The Apostle Paul tells us that he received this revelation concerning the mystery of Communion directly from Jesus (see 1 Corinthians 11:23-34). This should help us see that Communion is not peripheral. Christianity's greatest apostle and theologian received his eucharistic revelation from Christ himself! Communion is a major doctrine and central practice of Christian faith. At the center of Christian praxis we find a table. For the Christian, the holy of holies is the Communion table. No longer is the holiest of all a veiled chamber reserved for a solitary high priest, now it's a shared table to which all are invited. Jesus is responsible for this monumental change.

Throughout his ministry, Jesus exercised a radical hospitality in his table practice. Sinners were welcome to sit with God and share a meal, just like Abraham did under the oaks of Mamre (Genesis 18). On the night before his suffering Jesus gave the world a new table, a sacramental table. The synoptic gospels along with the Apostle Paul tell us that as Jesus sat with his disciples in the Upper

Room during the Last Supper, he took bread and said, "This is my body." He then took a cup of wine and said, "This is my blood…" (Matthew 26:26, 28). Flesh and blood given as bread and wine. This is the eucharistic mystery. Divine flesh and blood somehow given to us in common bread and wine. Wheat and vine. Grain and grape. Seen properly, this opens the door to a sacramental ontology—a way of seeing all creation and all labor as sacred. Looking through a eucharistic lens we discover that we live, not in a secular world, but a sacred world, a world where every tree can become a burning bush aflame with the presence of God.

A sense of the sacred may be what we need most of all right now. The church in Western Europe and North America is struggling with deep disappointment. We are disappointed with the failure of the Christendom project. The grand attempt to produce continents of Christian civilization through the apparatus of the state is either dead or dying. It appears that cultural secularism has already won in Western Europe and will win in North America (despite the determination of conservatives to fight to the bitter end in the ugliness of the "culture wars"). So we either deny what is happening, which is more easily done in America, or we angrily blame scapegoats, or we simply trudge along a bit sad about it all. The church in the post-Christendom West is walking the Emmaus road, confused and disappointed, just like those two disciples on the first Easter (see Luke 24:13-35). Of course, the point of the Emmaus road story was that the two disciples had misread everything. Their disappointment was a result of their wrong expectations. They expected a conventional king after the model of the Pharaohs and Caesars. They expected Jesus to be a war-waging Messiah like King David or Judah Maccabeus. With those expectations they saw Jesus as a "failed" Messiah—a peace-preaching Messiah who ended up being executed by the Romans. Instead of kingdom come, it was Christ crucified—a dead end. As far as Cleopas and the other disciple were concerned, the movement in which they had invested all their hopes and dreams had failed. There was nothing to do now but go back home. So they walked the Emmaus road carrying a load of soul-crushing disappointment. This is when Jesus came and walked with them "in another form" (Mark 16:12).

When Jesus in the guise of a wayfaring stranger joined the disappointed disciples and remarked upon their evident sadness, they explained how they had hoped that Jesus of Nazareth was the long-awaited Messiah, the one who would redeem Israel. But that was all over. Their hopes had been dashed when their would-be Messiah was condemned by the priests and crucified by the Romans. Their movement had failed and disappointment had settled in. This is when the stranger embarked upon a long discourse through Moses and the Prophets explaining how suffering and even death were not incompatible with Messiah entering into his glorious reign—in fact, the Scriptures had foretold this very thing. That Sunday afternoon walk to Emmaus was the ultimate Old Testament survey class.

As the sun was setting, the three travelers arrived at Emmaus. After first feigning that he would continue his journey alone, the stranger accepted an invitation to share a meal with the two disciples. As they sat together at table in the fading light of that first Easter, the stranger surprisingly assumed the role of host. He took the bread, spoke the ancient Jewish blessing, broke the bread, and, when he offered the bread…something astonishing happened!

For a fleeting moment the two disciples recognized the stranger as…Jesus! Then he vanished! *Poof!* Gone! But the bread Jesus had been holding in his hands fell to the table. The blessed, broken, and offered bread hit the table with an emphatic thump! Jesus had been recognized for an ephemeral instant, then he had vanished. But in his place the bread remained. *Don't miss that.* The bread remained! The two disciples rushed back to Jerusalem to announce the good news that Jesus was risen. "They told what had happened on the road, and how he was made known to them in the breaking of the bread" (Luke 24:35).

Here we behold the eucharistic mystery, the sacred mystery that after Easter Christ is with us in another form, in the blessed and broken bread. This is the point of the dramatic gesture at the climactic moment in the Emmaus road story—Jesus is present as bread on the table! Of course, this is a very different presence than what was anticipated by either the Emmaus road disciples or the heirs of Christendom.

> Jesus will not be with us as a means of conventional political power. Jesus will be with us as bread on the table. Christ is present as sacramental mystery, not political action committee.

What both wanted was a conventional king on a throne of political power. What they got was broken bread on the Communion table. The false hope for the kingdom of Christ to be one of conventional political power was always bound to disappoint those who fail to understand the true nature of this new kingdom, whether it's the Emmaus Road disciples, the architects of Christendom, or the modern-day Religious Right. Jesus will not be with us as a means of conventional political power. Jesus will be with us as bread on the table. Christ is present as sacramental mystery, not political action committee. Blessed are they who are not disappointed.

For those Christians who dreamed of shaping the culture through political pressure and legislative coercion, these are days of anger, frustration, and disappointment. That experiment has failed and it cannot be repeated. Christendom is dead. But Christ is alive! For those who are willing to enter the sacramental mystery of Christ present as bread on the table, these are days of new opportunity. Instead of thinking politically, we are learning to think sacramentally. The way forward is far less political and far more mystical. A generation ago the great Catholic theologian Karl Rahner famously predicted, "The devout Christian of the future will either be a 'mystic', one who has 'experienced' something, or he will cease to be anything at all."[2] The future of Christianity belongs to the Thomas Merton kind of Christian, not the heirs of Jerry Falwell. This should be seen as a welcome change. It is only our false hopes that are being disappointed in the death of Christendom. Jesus never intended to change the world through battlefields or voting booths. Jesus has always intended to transform the world one life at a time at a shared table. At the church I pastor we no longer hand out "Christian voting guides," but every Sunday we offer "the body of Christ broken for you."

I'm not the least bit angry or even disappointed that Christendom has failed and that we now live in what might be described as a secular age. For one thing, it may not be that our age is as much secular as it is simply post-Christendom. The church in the West is finally coming out from under the long shadow of Constantine and we're trying to figure out what comes next. We too are walking the Emmaus road, learning to recognize Jesus in another form. We no longer have political power. What we do have is the mystery of the Eucharist. We offer the world the bread and wine, the body and blood of Christ. That is more than enough! So today our sermons don't end with, "Go write your senator and lobby Washington." Our sermons end with, "Come to the table and share in the life of Christ." Christ is present with us. He is present in the Eucharist. He is bread on the table. This is enough. I am not disappointed. My heart burns within me.

In the mystery of the Eucharist, God in Christ chooses to make himself present to humanity by ordinary elements. Through grain and grape, we find Christ present in the world. But it's not unprocessed grain and grape that we find on the Communion table, it's bread and wine. Grain and grape come from God's good earth, but bread and wine are the result of human industry. Bread and wine come about through a cooperation of the human and the divine. And herein lies a beautiful mystery. If grain and grape made bread and wine can communicate the body and blood of Christ, this has enormous implications for all legitimate human labor and industry. The mystery of the Eucharist does nothing less than make all human labor sacred. For there to be the holy sacrament of Communion there must be grain and grape, wheat fields and vineyards, bakers and winemakers. Human labor becomes a sacrament, a farmer planting wheat, a vintner tending vines, a miller grinding wheat, a winemaker crushing grapes, a woman baking bread, a man making wine, a trucker hauling bread, a grocer selling wine. Who knows what bread or what wine might end up on the Communion table as the body and blood of Christ. This is where we discover the holy mystery that all labor necessary for human flourishing is sacred. A farmer plowing his field, a worker in a bakery, a trucker hauling goods, a grocer selling wares—all are engaged in work that is just as sacred as the priest or pastor serving Communion on Sunday. The Eucharist pulls back the curtain to reveal a sacramental world.

Don't over-scrutinize or over-literalize this eucharistic mystery. Don't try to miss the point. Don't get hung up on whether or not the labor is connected specifically with the production of grain and grape, bread and wine—the elements of Communion. That's not the point. The point is that all work necessary for human flourishing is not just legitimate, but sacramental. Indeed we are a "kingdom of priests" (Revelation 1:6, NLT) and "the kingdom of the world has become the kingdom of our Lord and his Messiah" (Revelation 11:15). What we may think of as routine and mundane is actually an engagement with the sacred. The mystery of the Eucharist reveals this to be so. Annie Dillard makes this point when she tells the story of buying the communion wine for her tiny church on Puget Sound:

> How can I buy the communion wine? Who am I to buy the communion wine? Someone has to buy the communion wine. Having wine instead of grape juice was my idea, and of course I offered to buy it. Shouldn't I be wearing robes and, especially, a mask? Shouldn't I *make* the communion wine? Are there holy grapes, is there holy ground? There are no holy grapes, there is no holy ground, nor is there anyone but us. I have an empty knapsack over my parka's shoulders; it is

cold, and I'll want my hands in my pockets. According to the Rule of St. Benedict, I should say, Our hands in our pockets. "All things come of thee, O Lord, and of thine own have we given thee." There must be a rule for the purchase of communion wine. "Will that be cash, or charge?" … And I'm out on the road again walking, my right hand forgetting my left. I'm out on the road again walking, and toting a backload of God. Here is a bottle of wine with a label, Christ with a cork. I bear holiness splintered into a vessel, very God of very God, the sempiternal silence personal and brooding, bright on the back of my ribs.[3]

We may live in a secular age, but our secular age lives and moves and has its being in a sacramental world. Our secular eyes may be too dim to see it, but that doesn't mean creation is not shining with the brightness of God. The light brighter than the sun on the Mount of Transfiguration testifies that flesh and blood can convey the glory of God. In our sometimes frenzied, sometimes wearied labors, we can become blind to the glory that is all around us. Like the joker said to the thief:

Businessmen, they drink my wine, plowmen dig my earth
None of them along the line know what any of it is worth
—Bob Dylan, "All Along The Watchtower"

But the Eucharist shows us the worth! God's good creation is holy enough to hold the life of God—whether it be a burning bush, a baby in Bethlehem, grain and grape, bread and wine. It's not a rare diamond or a magical elixir that communicates the life of Christ to us, but something as common, earthy, and ordinary as bread and wine. Every time we receive Communion we are reminded that we live in a sacramental world. The wheat fields of Kansas and the vineyards of California are as holy as chapels and cathedrals. God reveals himself not in inscrutable quatrains, but in grain and grape. The scent of God can be detected in the smell of a newborn baby and the sweat of a carpenter, in bread baking and wine fermenting. Secularism is not a state of being, it's only a way of misapprehending the world. If we walk the twenty-first century Emmaus road thinking God is absent and the mission has failed, we will be deeply disappointed. But if we can learn to recognize Jesus in another form and see him revealed in the breaking of bread, our hearts will burn with joy!

> We may live in a secular age, but our secular age lives and moves and has its being in a sacramental world.

> O God, whose blessed Son made himself known to his disciples in the breaking of bread: Open the eyes of our faith, that we may behold him in all his redeeming work; who lives and reigns with you, in the unity of the Holy Spirit, one God, now and forever. Amen.[4]

Feasts and banquets are Jesus' most common metaphor for the kingdom of God. When Jesus wasn't talking about a metaphorical table, he was often sitting down at a literal table. In Luke's Gospel alone there are nearly three dozen references to eating, drinking, and sitting at table. Throughout the third Gospel, Jesus is moving from meal to meal, table to table. Jesus is constantly announcing and enacting the kingdom of God by a common meal at a shared table. The most radical aspect of Jesus and his moveable feast was his penchant for sharing the table with all the "wrong" people—the sinner, the outcast, the excluded. In a culture where table practice was closely associated with personal holiness, this was bound to raise eyebrows...and it did. The scribes and Pharisees grumbled, "This fellow welcomes sinners and eats with them" (Luke 15:1). And Jesus was happy to live up to their criticism. Jesus was clearly willing to share the table with anyone who would come to him. For Jesus, a shared table was the way salvation came to sinners. When Jesus sat at table with Jericho's chief tax collector Zacchaeus, the meal was not over before the notorious sinner was saved. When Jesus was asked "Will only a few be saved?" he responded by saying "People will come from east and west, from north and south, and will eat in the kingdom of God" (Luke 13:23,29). For Jesus, salvation could be described as eating in the kingdom of God, and he anticipated all kinds of people coming to his table. In his preaching, parables, and practice Jesus made it clear that salvation and the kingdom of God are centered, not in a temple, but at a table. Jesus relocated the holy of holies from a veiled chamber reserved for a solitary high priest, to a shared table to which all are invited. Jesus overturned money-changing tables in the temple, but set up banqueting tables in his Father's house.

Prior to Jesus, the Jewish concept of holiness was one of ever smaller and ever holier concentric circles. As one moved closer to the holy of holies, access became more restricted. The land of Israel was the holy land within the world. Within the land of Israel was the holy city of Jerusalem. Within Jerusalem was the holy temple. Within the temple were increasing levels of holiness with corresponding restrictedness. There was a court for Jews only, where Gentiles were prohibited. A court for men only, where women were prohibited. A court for priests only, where laymen were prohibited. And at last, the holy of holies where only the high priest could enter, and only once a year. Holiness was something to be protected from the profane.

But Jesus changed all of that. Jesus reversed the concept of kosher. When the unclean touched Jesus, Jesus was not made unclean, rather the unclean were made whole. During Jesus' ministry sinners were given unfettered access to the holiest of all. What could be more holy than sitting at table and dipping bread in the same bowl with God himself? In the hospitality of Jesus we make the unprecedented discovery that God is willing to share his table with anyone—even with sinners. Especially with sinners. This fundamentally changes our idea of kosher. The apostle Peter eventually learns to say, "God has shown me that I should not call anyone profane or unclean" (Acts 10:28). For the Christian the holiest of all is the Communion table where we are offered the body and blood of Jesus. Instead of being restricted to a particular geography and limited to a priestly elite, the Christian holy of holies can be located anywhere and everywhere. The Lord's Table bears witness to the new covenant truth that the holy land is the whole earth and the chosen people are the human race.

During his final week of ministry in Jerusalem, Jesus did two highly significant things: He shut down the temple (albeit briefly) and inaugurated a table. The temple is protested while the table is blessed. During Holy Week, Jesus prophesied the demise of the temple and the rise of the table. Jesus shifts our thinking from temple to table. As Jesus sat at the table with his disciples during the last supper, he told them he would not drink from the fruit of the vine until he drank it with them anew in the coming kingdom of God (see Matthew 26:29, Mark 14:25, Luke 22:18, 28). This explains why Jesus was so eager to eat and drink with his disciples after his resurrection—he was celebrating with them the coming of the Father's kingdom. In the Book of Acts Peter described the apostles as those who "ate and drank with him after he rose from the dead" (Acts

> We thought God was a deity in a temple. It turns out God is a father at a table.

10:41). The risen Christ did not appear at the temple but at meal tables. The center of God's activity had shifted—it was no longer the temple but the table that was the holiest of all. The church would do well to think of itself, not so much as a kind of temple, but as a kind of table. This represents a fundamental shift. Consider the difference between temple and table—temple is exclusive; table is inclusive. Temple is hierarchical; table is egalitarian. Temple is authoritarian; table is affirming. Temple is uptight and status conscious. Table is relaxed and "family-style." Temple is a rigorous enforcement of purity codes that prohibits the unclean. Table is a welcome home party celebrating the return of sinners. The temple was temporal. The table is eternal. We thought God was a deity in a temple. It turns out God is a father at a table.

Communion was not an invention of Jesus, it was an innovation of Jesus. It was obviously based on the Jewish Passover meal, but it was reimagined. Instead of remembering the Passover, it would remember a new salvation story, a new exodus. Salvation history would now take on a global scope. This new memorial meal would include the Jewish Passover, but it would also encompass other liberation stories. Yahweh would be worshiped as the God who brought the Hebrews out of Egypt, but also as the God who brought "the Philistines from Caphtor and the Syrians from Kir" (Amos 9:7, ESV). No longer would the covenant meal be restricted to a particular ethnicity or nationality—now "many will come from east and west and will eat with Abraham and Isaac and Jacob in the kingdom of heaven" (Matthew 8:11). The exclusivity of the temple is giving way to the inclusivity of the table. The difference between the old and the new, temple and table, is like the difference between performing purity rites under the judgmental gaze of religious gatekeepers and sharing food and drink at table with close friends. Instead of the temple method of declaring the outsider unclean and restricting their access, at the Lord's Table we say, "Pull up a chair and sit with us, we'll make room for you." In the temple the sacred is preserved by the practice of exclusion—women, Gentiles, sinners, and the unclean are kept at a proscribed distance. At the table the sacred is expressed in the practice of inclusion—receiving the outsider and unclean for whom Jesus always makes room.

Like the other Gospel writers, John recounts the story of Jesus multiplying the loaves and fishes to feed five thousand. But John adds this unique postscript, "When Jesus realized that they were about to come and take him by force to make him king, he withdrew again to the mountain by himself" (John 6:15). The crowd's response to this "table in the wilderness" (Psalm 78:19) was an impulse to make Jesus king...but Jesus declined. Why? Jesus is king, he came to be king, king is what Messiah means. So why does Jesus slip away from the crowd when they want to make him king? The issue is force. The crowd wanted to "take him by *force* and make him king." At the center of the crowd's concept of kingship was violent force. They wanted to *force* Jesus to be their *forceful* king so he could lead their *forces* in an uprising of violent *force* against the Romans. This was antithetical to the kind of king Jesus came to be. Caesar is a crucifying king who reigns by force. Christ is the crucified king who reigns without force. Christ's kingdom is built upon co-suffering love, not violent force.

The crowd that wanted to force Jesus to be king was operating from the dominant paradigm of scarcity. This is the paradigm that possessed Cain to kill Abel, and it lies at the dark heart of human civilization. We are scripted to believe that reality is zero-based and that we live in a closed system. This paradigm of scarcity and insufficiency is the philosophy that undergirds our structures of systemic sin. We fear there won't be enough land, water, food, oil, money, labor to go around, so we build evil structures of sinful force to guarantee that those we call "us" will have what we call "ours." We call it security. We call it defense. We call it freedom. What we don't call it is what it is...fear. Driven by our fear of scarcity we create an organized, large-scale, slow-motion version of anarchy. A mob on a looting and killing rampage is called anarchy. European colonists looting and killing indigenous people is called glorious conquest—but it's just looting and murder on a grand scale. Kings are tasked with looting our enemies on our behalf.

> They say that patriotism is the last refuge
> To which a scoundrel clings

> Steal a little and they throw you in jail
> Steal a lot and they make you king
> —Bob Dylan, "Sweetheart Like You"

How else are we to understand the wars of conquest in the light of Christ? In the American context the native peoples were the victims of the organized, large-scale, slow motion version of anarchy called Manifest Destiny. The paradigm of scarcity is absolutely dominant in the mind of fallen mankind. So we are committed to furthering economic self-interest through force. This is how we understand the role of kings (or presidents). This leads to competition, conflict, conquest, resentment, rebellion, retaliation, and war, which in turn tragically leads to the self-fulfilling prophecy of scarcity and lack. These are the four horseman of the Apocalypse that keep galloping across history. The white horse of conquest, followed by the red horse of war, followed by the black horse of famine, followed by the pale horse of death. Put it on repeat and you have world history. Jesus is the king who comes to save humanity from the stupid cycle of conquest, war, famine, and death. So when the crowd tried to force Jesus onto the white horse of violent conquest, he refused.

The miracle of the loaves and fishes was intended to be a sign pointing us to a new paradigm. Jesus was constantly teaching people not to worry about scarcity, but to trust in God. Jesus wants us to see that we don't live in a closed universe; reality is not zero-based. Instead God breaks into our world with the beauty of the infinite, to borrow a phrase from David Bentley Hart. The sign of the loaves and fishes was intended to show that with God all things are possible, and that the paradigm of scarcity is a satanic lie.

When the Galilean crowd failed to get this message, but instead wanted to use Jesus to start the cycle of conquest, war, famine, and death—those hideous horsemen—Jesus withdrew to the mountain for a night of prayer. The next day Jesus took a different approach with the crowd:

> When they found him on the other side of the sea, they said to him, "Rabbi, when did you come here?" Jesus answered them, "Very truly, I tell you, you are looking for me, not because you saw signs, but because you ate your fill of the loaves. Do not work for the food that perishes, but for the food that endures for eternal life, which the Son of Man will give you. For it is on him that God the Father has set his seal....I am the living bread that came down from heaven. Whoever eats of this bread will live forever; and the bread that I will give for the life of the world is my flesh." The Jews then disputed among themselves, saying, "How can this man give us his flesh to eat?" So Jesus said to them, "Very truly, I tell you, unless you eat the flesh of the Son of Man and drink his blood, you have no life in you." (John 6:25–27; 51–53)

Instead of a battlefield where the four horsemen of the Apocalypse ride in vicious repetition, Jesus calls the world to a table where he offers humanity his flesh and blood. And why? Because to eat the flesh and drink the blood of Jesus is to ingest the infinite. Jesus said it this way, "Those who eat my flesh and drink my blood have eternal life" (John 6:54). Jesus abandons the worn-out way of trying to change the world by riding warhorses across battlefields. That will never change the world. That's the way the world already is. Instead Jesus calls us to a table and asks us to eat his flesh and drink his blood that we might participate in his eternal life. But the Galilean crowd was offended by Jesus' provocative flesh-eating and blood-drinking invitation.

It is significant that Jesus never softens the scandal of his invitation by saying, "I mean symbolically." No, Jesus just keeps intensifying his eucharistic theology by saying, "My flesh is true food and my blood is true drink. Those who eat my flesh and drink my blood abide in me, and I in them" (John 6:55–56). Even when many disciples complained, "This teaching is difficult; who can accept it?" (John 6:60), Jesus doesn't relent. And what was the result? "Because of this many of his disciples turned back and no longer went about with him" (John 6:66). This abandoned discipleship is sad, but for Jesus, the idea that his followers would feed on his flesh and drink his blood was a nonnegotiable. If we try to remove the scandal of a robust eucharistic theology by reducing it all to mere symbol, we are doing the very thing Jesus refused to do. Let the scandal remain. We are invited to eat the flesh and drink the blood of God that we might participate in eternal life. The most appropriate response to this holy mystery is not an empiricist explanation or an embarrassed backpedaling, but a reverent amen. When the officiant says, "The body of Christ broken for you," the communicant says, "Amen." It is the beauty of the infinite offered in the Eucharist that saves us from the fear that unleashes the four horsemen of the Apocalypse.

A young woman I know, the daughter of a friend, grew up in a charismatic church where her father is the pastor. In her teen years her Christian faith began to waver. The evangelical Christianity she had grown up with didn't seem thick enough to sustain her as she moved into adulthood. She was passing through the kind of crisis that is often the demise of Christian faith for too many young evangelicals. Happily, while attending college her faith revived. But it wasn't a return to thin evangelicalism, it was an embrace of the Great Tradition—the creeds and sacraments of historic Christianity. Her faith was now buttressed by serious theology and sacred mystery. Her father heard me speak at a pastors' conference where I was addressing the need for evangelical churches to recover the practice of weekly Communion. After my presentation he approached me and said, "Now I know what my daughter means when she asks, 'What is church without the Eucharist?'"

Indeed, what is church without the Eucharist? It's an insightful and important question. In a very real sense the church is the ecclesial body of Christ sustained by the sacramental body of Christ. Week by week we feed upon the flesh and blood of Christ that we might be an incarnation of the flesh and blood of Christ within the world. "This is a great mystery, and I am applying it to Christ and the church" (Ephesians 5:32). This is why for most of church history the sacrament, not the sermon, has been the central aspect of Christian worship. Christian faith is more about connecting our lives with Christ than it is about gaining spiritual information. Making church more about the sermon than the sacrament is a move toward secularism. (And this is coming from someone who has written over three thousand sermons and loves to preach!) To resist the secularizing of Christianity we need a more

sacramental worship. What the sacrament of Communion does
that the sermon cannot do is offer the worshiper a direct encounter
with the life of Christ. Jesus is still saying, "Take, eat; this is my
body" (Matthew 26:26). Grain and grape. Wheat and vine. Bread
and wine. Flesh and blood. It's the Eucharist that teaches us how to
belong to God's good world—a world that is more sacred than we
ever dreamed.

Belong
(Antidote for Gnosticism)

> Let Christ inform all of life
> Don't be a religious cliché
> Be a real human being
> Belong to the human race
> Belong to the woods
> Belong to the city
> Go for long walks
> Learn to appreciate art
> Take up the violin
> Cultivate culinary skills
> Read War and Peace
> Laugh more than you do
> Weep now and then
> Listen to live jazz
> Pray
> Eat a peach
> Do something ridiculous
> Go dancing

Stop judging
Start loving
Plant a garden
Climb a mountain
Memorize a long poem
Learn some astronomy
Become a bee-keeper
Go back to college
Take up a new hobby
Make some new friends
Read the Bible
In a new translation
Get rid of bumper stickers
Learn a foreign language
Watch a foreign film
Change your mind
Drink only good coffee
Trust the *sommelier*
Talk to your neighbor
Not about religion
Go to church
Go to the circus
Don't confuse them
Be human
Belong

Chapter 8

Every Grain of Sand

I don't think it is enough appreciated how much an outdoor book the Bible is. … It is best read and understood outdoors, and the farther outdoors the better. Or that has been my experience of it. Passages that within walls seem improbable or incredible, outdoors seem merely natural. This is because outdoors we are confronted everywhere with wonders; we see that the miraculous is not extraordinary but the common mode of existence. It is our daily bread. Whoever really has considered the lilies of the field or the birds of the air and pondered the improbability of their existence in this warm world within the cold and empty stellar distances will hardly balk at the turning of water into wine—which was, after all, a very small miracle. We forget the greater and still continuing miracle by which water (with soil and sunlight) is turned into grapes.

—Wendell Berry[1]

I was born and raised in the flatlands of the Midwest and was thirty years old before I saw any real mountains. But when I did, it was love at first sight. I remember thinking, "Where have you been all my life?" It was autumn in the Rocky Mountains and Peri and I were driving in the Sawatch Range of Colorado. The elk were bugling, the aspens were on fire, and the first snows had already fallen. As we drove I was mesmerized by the snowy peaks. I wanted to climb them all. At some point we impulsively pulled over and began a scramble up some unnamed peak. By the time we reached the top we were in a blizzard. We made our way down the mountain and back to the car in near white-out conditions. Looking back from the vantage point of experience, our little adventure verged on the foolhardy, but I couldn't help myself.

Today I call the great peaks in Rocky Mountain National Park my friends. Longs, Meeker, Pagoda, McHenrys, Chiefs Head, Hallet, Otis, Taylor, Chapin, Chiquita, Ypsilon, and all the rest. I know them by name. I know their faces, their moods, their proclivities. If I don't see them for awhile, I feel their absence. It's not just the beauty of their grandeur or the challenge of climbing them that draws me to them, I also love their wildness. I love the mountains for the same reason I love the oceans and forests and deserts—they are wild. They are untamed. They are as they are intended, which is to say, holy. And their wild holiness has healing properties. When I say the wilderness has healing properties, I mean that quite seriously. The oceans, deserts, forests, and mountains are medicinal; they are a tonic to the mind, a palliative to the soul.

We are indigenous to the dirt. We are humans from the humus. We are a mysterious synthesis of the dust of the earth and the breath of God.

Humanity did not spring fully formed from the head of Zeus like Athena or fall from the sky like one of the gods of Greek mythology. Humanity did not have a pre-existent state in the non-spatial, non-temporal realm of perfect forms as Plato imagined.

Humanity did not come from somewhere other than the earth. Humanity's only home has been the spinning blue orb third from the sun. If this world is not our home (as the Gnostics claimed), then we are homeless. We have a native connectedness to this creation that cannot be severed without suffering ill consequences. We are indigenous to the dirt. We are humans from the humus. We are a mysterious synthesis of the dust of the earth and the breath of God. To be too separated from unmolested nature tends toward a pathology of the soul. We cannot always have concrete beneath our feet; sometimes we need sand between our toes. We cannot always be illuminated by fluorescent glow; sometimes we need to be bathed in cold starlight. There are times when the best therapy for a troubled mind is nothing more than a long walk in the woods. Mountains are my medicine.

After 2004 and our embarking upon the Great Migration toward a more substantive, more beautiful, more mysterious Christianity, the ensuing criticism from fundamentalist-leaning church members began to take its toll. The wolf of depression seemed always to be prowling near my door. That's when Peri and I learned just how healing a few days in the mountains can be. Settling into the steady rhythm of a long hike, noticing the wonder of green lichen growing on gray granite, contemplating the impassivity of the mountains to the cruel vagaries of life—these were the things that restored my soul and kept the wolf at bay. I also began to notice that I did my best thinking and praying in the high tundra. The expansive vista seemed to help my soul expand— to think more broadly, to pray more generously. On the high tundra beneath the big sky a petty theology of a small and capricious God appears as ludicrous as it is. It's probably dangerous to do all of our theology in the close quarters of indoors. Theologians need to be outdoorsmen.

We come from the earth. Our sacred scriptures tell us that God formed humankind from the humus of earth. *Adam* (humankind) came from the *adamah* (ground). We are soil with a soul. This is the common ancestry we share with all of creation— with mountains and marmots, with algae and orangutans, lichen and leopards. We belong to the outdoors. Long before our history was written in books it was written in nature. We are stardust and we are children of God. To pit one against the other is a foolish mistake. We are children of God whom the Creator has drawn forth from the earth. This is why we have an affinity with all of God's good creation. All things are connected. Humanity is not something foreign to nature, we fully belong to it. When I hike in the mountains I am not an alien or an intruder; I am in my natural habitat. I belong there. But I must be there in gentleness and respect. I don't own creation, I simply belong to it, and I will treat it with due reverence.

We humans are kin to the deer. And sometimes I think they perceive more than we do. Like Yellow Calf, the aged and blind Indian in *Winter in the Blood* said, "They can tell by the moon when the world is cockeyed. ... Of course men are the last to know."[2] But are humans in some way special or are we just the smartest mammal on the block? This is where the sacred wisdom of Genesis takes us beyond the limits of empirical science. I have no arguments with the consensus of peer-reviewed science. I thrill in their discoveries. I merely insist that when empiricism has said all it can say, there is still more to be said. The Scriptures give voice to the Spirit-inspired mystics who peered into the deeper meaning beyond mere matter and sheer existence. The witness of science and the witness of faith need not be an argument with one another. They are simply two different languages addressing different kinds of questions. So the ancient wisdom of Genesis reveals that the God who said, "Let there be light," also said, "Let there be life," and finally said, "Let there be those like Us." This is a deep mystery, but the capacity for self-awareness is related to the gift of God-consciousness. When God breathed upon our ancestors, animate creatures formed from the dust of the earth, they became human, which is to say they possessed the capacity to contemplate their own existence, seek intimacy with their Creator, and bear the divine image within creation. The impulse to seek after God is intrinsic to human nature and is perhaps our most human instinct. Humans are the God-marked, God-obsessed being.

The celebration of natural creation is entirely compatible with Christian spirituality. We cannot love the Creator and be dismissive or abusive toward his creation. T.S. Eliot said, "A wrong attitude toward nature implies, somewhere, a wrong attitude toward God."[3] I couldn't agree more. I'm always more of a mystic when I'm in the mountains. Poetry comes to me unbeckoned in the mountains—it just flows. Not long ago I stepped out of a mountain cabin and laid on the ground to gaze in wide-eyed wonder at the Milky Way in the clear Colorado sky. This is the prayer that moment evoked.

Stars

I don't spend enough time looking at stars
I'm a modern man, with a roof over my head
I live in a world of ambient light and washed-out night skies
That's one reason why there's not enough wonder in our eyes

Tonight I saw the stars from the crisp Colorado skies
The cluster of the Pleiades and the cords of Orion
And I said—
The world is old
The stars are older still
They twinkle, but they don't blink
They're impassive (I think)

And I wonder—
Do they watch the goings-on of the blue marble below?
Do the twinkling but not blinking stars think
Will those curious little creatures ever get it together?
Will they ever figure out they're all in it together?
Will it ever dawn on them that they're children of God?
Will they ever learn that in the long run—
There is no them, there is only us?

I wonder if they wonder about us
After all, the song is right—
We are stardust, we are golden
We are billion year old carbon
We've got to get ourselves back to the garden
Yes, we do—we've got to!
(The bombs are now far too big for us not to!)

I looked at the stars tonight
And I prayed a prayer—
God, I don't know what will happen tomorrow
I don't know what will be a billion centuries on

But I believe in you
You are the True, the Good, the Beautiful
You sustain your finite creation from your infinite being

O beautiful Infinite
Forgive us. Restore us. Heal us. Help us. Save us. Please!
Yes! I believe you will!
For—
Christ has died, Christ is risen, Christ will come again

And so anon or much later on…
Everything will be alright—
In the end we'll find the lost garden
And learn to love our brother
We'll walk with you again
Or for the first time
And shine like the stars
Forever

I had a dream. I dreamed I was riding a yellow bicycle. While riding my yellow bicycle I was intently observing the beauty of creation, and especially the vibrant colors—the green of the grass and trees (the human eye is more attune to the green spectrum than any other), the blue sky, the red roses, the yellow dandelions. During my colorful dreamland bike ride I was thinking about the nature of salvation. When I awoke I wrote down my nocturnal thoughts: When we make salvation mostly postmortem, all about the afterlife, we create a barrier—a wall of separation between redemption and the land of the living. No wonder so many shrug their shoulders in disinterest. But when we locate salvation here and now, people are naturally interested. Salvation is about being human. This is why the Word became flesh—human flesh. Jesus came to give us back the life we lost ever since we stumbled out of the garden to wander in the violent land east of Eden.

When Adam and Eve were banished from Eden, creation lost its gardener. Is it any surprise that the faster our technology has advanced, the more rapacious we have become in the pillage and plunder of our planet? When we lost our vocation as gardeners, the planet lost its God-ordained caretakers. From the Stone Age to the dawn of the Industrial Age the planet has been able to muddle by without its caretakers, but now human civilization, divorced from its original vocation, threatens to imperil the earth. Mary Magdalene's Easter "mistake" of thinking Jesus was the gardener is a poetic hint of how the Last Adam leads us back to our first vocation. Any understanding of salvation that doesn't lead us to love God's creation is far more Gnostic than Christian. Or perhaps it's just voracious capitalism dressed up in Christian garb—a wolf in sheep's clothing. If we cannot love the primeval forest, I'm not sure we can love either God or neighbor. The wise Elder Zosima in *The Brothers Karamazov* gives this counsel to the novice monk Alyosha:

> Love all of God's creation, both the whole of it and every grain of sand. Love every leaf, every ray of God's light. Love animals, love plants, love each thing. If you love each thing, you will perceive the mystery of God in things. Once you have perceived it, you will begin tirelessly to perceive more and more of it every day. And you will come

at last to love the whole world with an entire, universal love.[4]

If someone says that sounds like tree-hugger theology, I say a theologian can do worse than to hug a tree.

In the fury of the moment I can see the Master's hand
In every leaf that trembles, in every grain of sand
—Bob Dylan, "Every Grain of Sand"

When Karl Rahner predicted that "the devout Christian of the future will either be a mystic or he will cease to be anything at all" he was keenly prescient. Indeed, the hope for a vibrant Christianity in the West lies, in part, in a recovery of mysticism. The tyranny of empiricism so characteristic of modernity is at last coming to an end. A Christianity that has no room for the mystics can expect to be increasingly ignored, left to molder in its own arrogant assumptions. The rise of global Pentecostalism in the twentieth century is just one portent of the type of spirituality that is capable of addressing the spiritual hunger of the postmodern world. Of course there was a time when mysticism was not tangential to Christianity but an integral aspect of Christian experience. After all, we Christians claim it is possible to communicate with God, that miracles are credible, and that the rightful ruler of our planet is a man who was raised from the dead after being crucified two thousand years ago. Mysticism is no outlier to orthodox Christianity. We worship the one who turns water into wine.

We are witnessing today an increasing interest in what might be described as aboriginal spirituality. From the point of view of

Christian theology, aboriginal spirituality is not heterodox, but simply a spirituality rooted in something other than the European Enlightenment—a spirituality not of the ivory tower, but of the moss-covered forest. Today most of us have enough good sense to lament that Christianity arrived in the "new" world as a stowaway in the company of gold-crazed Spanish conquistadors and English pilgrims driven to cruelty by the lie of Manifest Destiny. But what if it had been different? What if there had been a genuine exchange of ideas, a gracious cultural cross-pollination? How much richer might Western spirituality be today if this had occurred? Or do we still cling to the lie of a European hegemony in all things, including spirituality? Simply because Europeans had the advantage of better immune systems, steel weapons, and the will to weaponize gunpowder doesn't mean Europeans had superior spiritual instincts.

Because of a twist of geographical fate, Europeans had the advantage of an earlier reception of the gospel and access to the Hebrew and Christian Scriptures. But by the time Columbus made his blundering "discovery," Europeans had also lost much of their aboriginal wisdom—which is to say, they had forgotten that humans belong to the earth. Europeans had learned how to dominate nature, but not how to live with nature. Half a millennium of that trajectory has left our planet in peril. Perhaps, while there is still time, we should become humble enough to consult the wisdom of those who knew how to live in respectful relationship with the rest of God's creation. This was the instinct of Saint Francis, the spiritual savant who spoke of Brother Sun and Sister Moon, Brother Fire and Sister Water. It's this type of integrated spirituality—Christian theology and aboriginal wisdom—that compels me to read both the Swiss theologian Karl

Barth and the Native American poet John Trudell. I benefit from both.

With Western culture exhibiting so clearly the symptoms of a deep spiritual malaise, a poverty of soul that is harming both people and planet, we need to bring an end to European hubris. Maybe with chastened humility we could ask if cultures who have lived in close harmony with creation for thousands of years can teach us how to become custodians instead of conquistadors, participants instead of plunderers. For in plundering the planet we have pillaged our souls, leaving us with an emptiness that systematic theology alone cannot fill. So mysticism beckons. We have our scriptures; we have our creeds. These are sufficient to keep us safely within Christian orthodoxy. But can we also learn to listen to the wise poets and sages of aboriginal spirituality who can teach us much that has been forgotten? I hope so. Because secularism, which appears to be the only other alternative, leads to nothing but a spiritual dead end. Either we become mystics, or it won't be long before we are nothing at all. And as I said, I'm always more of a mystic when I'm in the mountains.

The Bible opens with a creation narrative, and the constant refrain is the goodness of it all. In the first chapter of Genesis God declares every day as good. The third day (the day life begins) is declared good twice. On the sixth day of creation we are told, "God saw everything that he had made, and indeed, it was very good" (Genesis 1:31). The ancient Hebrew account of the entire goodness of creation stands in stark contrast to the pagan creation stories where the world comes into existence amidst the chaos of a great struggle between good and evil. In the rival myths of the ancient world, evil plays a role in creation. The first great revelation of the Hebrew scriptures is that the universe flows entirely from the goodness of God; evil played no part in God's good creation.

Genesis also takes us beyond where science can go. Astrophysicists can quite accurately trace the beginning of time back 13.7 billion years to the "let there be light" moment known as the Big Bang. But beyond that they cannot go. Anything prior to energy and matter (and the "time" which matter and energy create) is an impenetrable barrier for empiricism. Which is why Ludwig Wittgenstein concludes his *Tractatus Logico-Philosophicus* by famously saying, "What we cannot speak about we must pass over in silence."[5] Wittgenstein understood that there can never be a purely scientific answer to this fundamental question: Why is there something instead of nothing? Any attempt to answer this grand question broaches upon the philosophical or, more accurately, the religious.

The great monotheistic faiths have always answered the question of why there is something instead of nothing in the same way, the only way it can be answered: GOD. "In the beginning God created the heavens and the earth" (Genesis 1:1). But why? Why did God bother? Why did God create? Why did God say, "Let there be"? The mystics have always given the same answer—because God is love, love seeking expression. From what the Cappadocian Fathers called the *perichoresis*—the eternal dance that is Father, Son, and Holy Spirit, there burst forth an explosion of love. Some call it the Big Bang. Some call it Genesis. If you like we can call it the genesis of love as light and all that is. What is light? God's love in the form of photons. What is water? A liquid expression of God's love. What is a mountain? God's love in granite, so much older than human sorrow. What is a tree? God's love growing up from the ground. What is a bull moose? God's love sporting spectacular antlers. What is a whale? Fifty tons of

God's love swimming in the ocean. As we learn to look at creation as goodness flowing from God's own love, we begin to see the sacredness of all things, or as Dostoevsky and Dylan said, in every grain of sand. All of creation is a gift—a gift flowing from the self-giving love of God.

Why are there light and oceans and trees and moose and whales and every grain of sand? Because God is love—love that seeks expression in self-giving creativity. Unless we understand this we will misunderstand everything, and in our misunderstanding we will harm creation, including our fellow image-bearing sisters and brothers. Existence only makes sense when it is seen through the lens of love. At the beginning of time there is love. At the bottom of the universe there is love. Admittedly freedom allows for other things too—from cancer cells to atomic bombs—but at the bottom of the universe it's love all the way down. Cancer cells and atomic bombs will not have the final word. At the end of things there is love. When the last star burns out, God's love will be there for whatever comes after. In the end it all adds up to love. So when calculating the meaning of life, if it doesn't add up to love, go back and recalculate, because you've made a serious mistake. As Terrance Malick says in his *Tree of Life,* perhaps the greatest film ever made, "Unless you love, your life will flash by." Love alone gives meaning to our fleeting fourscore sojourn.

Religion has always been about the search for meaning, and as long as it follows the path of love, it's on the right track. But sadly, the first thing Adam (humankind) said was this, "I heard the sound of you in the garden, and I was afraid, because I was naked, and I hid myself" (Genesis 3:10). In the shame of our nakedness we are afraid of God and hide from him. Our perfect fear casts out all love. And so we try to find some meaning for life apart from love, but it always leads to disaster and dead ends. In our primitive dread we imagine a God who is petulant and hard to please, vindictive and retributive, capricious and cruel. But these are only petty projections born of our own fear. The mystics have always know better. On the great expanse of the high tundra between Longs Peak and the Never Summer Mountains I know better. God is love. When I remember this (and it's too easily forgotten), I'm reminded that I can afford to love, because love goes with the grain of the universe. The "wrath of God" is but one way of describing the shards of suffering we inevitably subject ourselves to when we go against the grain of God's love. God is all love, but we have to go with the grain of love or suffer the pain of self-inflicted sorrow. I think Elder Zosima is right when he says, "I ask myself: 'What is hell?' And I answer thus: 'Hell is the suffering of being no longer able to love.'"[6] Zosima then goes on to describe the plight of those who refuse to understand love as the meaning of life:

> In Jesus' parable, the rich man ends up in hell, not because he failed to believe the right things, but because he failed to love Lazarus.

> They are insatiable unto ages of ages, and reject forgiveness, and curse God who calls to them. They cannot look upon the living God without hatred, and demand that there be no God of life, that God destroy himself with all of his creation.

And they will burn eternally in the fire of their
wrath, thirsting for death and nonexistence.[7]

To reject love as the meaning of existence is to long for
nonexistence. The refusal of love is to hate being itself. If we hate
being itself, we are consumed in the fire of our own wrath. Either we
love or we punish our own existence. Think about the pictures of
judgment given to us by Jesus in the Gospels. What is the criteria of
judgment? Love, always love. In Jesus' parable, the rich man ends up
in hell, not because he failed to believe the right things, but because he
failed to love Lazarus. For all we know the rich man had impeccable
theology. What he lacked was love. In the parable of the sheep and
goats, the goats are not condemned for wrong belief or for failing to
pray a sinner's prayer, but for failing to love the poor, the sick, the
immigrant, and the imprisoned. If Jesus is to be trusted, it seems we
will not be judged by how rightly we believed, but by how well we
loved. The judgment seat of Christ is not a theology quiz, but an
evaluation of love. If we assume the criteria of judgment is something
other than love, we are taking a huge risk. This is why Jesus taught that
the commandments are fulfilled by loving God and neighbor (see
Matthew 22:34–40). This is why Paul said that if we get everything
else right, but get love wrong, we get it *all* wrong (see 1 Corinthians
13). This is why Augustine said, "Love, and do what thou wilt."[8] No
one who loves ever comes to a bad end.

Could I have spoken so boldly about the supremacy of love
prior to 2004? I don't think so. I hadn't yet met the mystics. I
hadn't yet learned how to read the Bible contemplatively. I had too
much invested in proving that my tribe had all the right answers. I
would have to go on a journey before I could arrive at the place

where I really understood that the greatest of all is love. But by August of 2004 I was beginning that journey. That was the month Dallas Willard showed me the divine conspiracy. That was the month I packed my bags and left consumer Christianity behind. That was the month the Five Words were given to me. That was also the month that Peri and I had our worst day in the mountains. Though I could not understand it at the time, that episode in the Mummy Range was a prophetic metaphor of the journey we were just beginning. It happened like this…

We were on our annual summer vacation in Rocky Mountain National Park and we had decided on a long hike to the summit of three peaks in the Mummy Range, two of them above 13,000 feet—Chapin, Chiquita, and Ypsilon. We started at dawn and made good time. Around eleven in the morning we were headed up the third peak when we noticed the skies beginning to grow black. Still, we thought if we hurried we could get to the summit and back to the relative safety of tree line ahead of the storm. We were wrong. We were only ten minutes from the summit of Ypsilon when it became clear that we needed to turn around. We donned our rain gear and headed down—not the way we had come, but the most direct route to a lower elevation. Soon thunderbolts were crashing around us as we were pummeled by hail. It was a scary situation. And things got worse. In our haste we had descended into some nasty cliffs—Peri calls them the cliffs of insanity. I still remember her tears as we had to negotiate some difficult moves; she was convinced that one of us would fall to our doom. Finally after an arduous descent down a talus slope in freezing rain, we reached tree line. Now all we had to do was hike out. That turned out to be a problem.

For some reason I was convinced there was a trail nearby that would lead us back to the trailhead. I was mistaken. After wandering around for too long looking for a nonexistent trail, we eventually realized that we would have to navigate through the forest as best we could. We consulted map and compass and chose a heading, but bushwhacking through a mountain forest during a steady downpour of freezing rain is no easy thing. We were cold and making slow progress. At one point we considered the distinct possibility that we might have to spend an unplanned night in the mountains during what turned out to be, not an afternoon thunderstorm, but a major weather system. I remember crossing streams and fallen trees that seemed to be without end. I remember feeling like we were going the wrong way, even when the map and compass said we weren't. I remember being fearfully cold. Hours later we came to a clearing and made our way up a steep slope. I was convinced that the trail was at the top of the clearing. When we reached the top of the clearing and found no trail, I was completely dejected. Peri suggested that we pray. So we did. I then decided to climb to the top of the steep ridge and see if I could get my bearings. I hadn't climbed fifty feet when, there it was—the trail! Our wandering in the wilderness was over.

Today it's strange how we look back upon that day with a kind of fondness. It was difficult, it was scary, at times it was a bit dangerous, but still we remember it fondly. I said it was our worst day in the mountains, but it really wasn't. In some ways it was one of our best days. Despite our doubts at the time, we did the right things. Sometimes Peri will refer to that day as the time we were lost in the mountains. But we were never lost. We were not wandering around aimlessly. We had plotted a course with map and compass and stuck to it. We moved resolutely toward our goal, even if at times it didn't feel like it. Even if at times we doubted ourselves. We relied on our map and compass and found our way home.

Our difficult day in the Mummy Range is an apt metaphor for the journey we were beginning in that pivotal month of August of 2004. We would endure thunderbolts of criticism. We would shiver in the freezing rain of rejection. We would be plagued by moments of self doubt. But we would do the right thing. At times we would feel like we were on the cliffs of insanity holding on by our fingernails. But God had given us a word. Five words. Cross, mystery, eclectic, community, revolution. This was our map and compass to lead through the woods of discontent and home to the deeper, richer Christianity we longed for. I don't regret that difficult day in the mountains. I don't regret the difficult spiritual journey we had begun. Life is a journey. Faith is a journey. We cannot make spiritual progress if we stay tethered to our certitude like the nervous tourist who dares not venture beyond the parking lot.

"The mountains are calling and I must go."
–John Muir

Deep Time
1, 2, 3, 4, 5, 6, 7, 8, 9, 10, 11, 12, 13, and 8/10—
Thousands of Millions of Years ago…
A silent singularity
Pregnant
Waiting

(Of course, it cannot "wait"—there is no motion, space, or time)
BANG!
Light and Heat and Expansion
ALL set in motion
Gravity did the rest
Galaxies and Quarks
(I cannot comprehend)
We have a Universe!
1, 2, 3, 4, and 1/2—
Thousands of Millions of Years ago…
It comes together, it spins, blue and green
We have a home!
For the miracle of Life
Amino acids
Single cells
Life in the sea
Arriving on land
The cold blooded rule
A rock falls from the sky
Gives the warm blooded a chance
Living in the trees
Venturing to the ground
Running down prey
To fuel a bigger brain
And finally the—
AWAKENING!
Not only being, not only alive, not only aware—
But aware of awareness
Self-consciousness

God-consciousness
Speaking of God
Did you know me way back when?
Or are you so immersed in the Story that I was a surprise even to
you?
What are the chances of the exact me coming to be—
When at the bottom of being there are tumbling dice?
Always planned or happy accident
Either way, I'm fine with it
It's enough that the I Am knows
That I am too
But this matter of deep time
It tells me something about you—
You are
Patient
So patient
All that is holy is patient
Love, Peace, Life
All that is unholy is impatient
sin, war, me
Help me to be holy
By being patient
Like you
With time—
Deep time, future time, all time
On your side
Amen

Chapter 9

❧

Come With Me

Sometimes the light's all shinin' on me
Other times I can barely see
Lately it occurs to me
What a long strange trip it's been
—The Grateful Dead, "Truckin'"

I n George MacDonald's enigmatic novel *Lilith* (a book that was enormously influential for both C.S. Lewis and J.R.R. Tolkien), there is a scene I often think about. The birdlike guide Mr. Raven is seeking to lead Mr. Vane on the journey he needs to take, a journey of suffering and salvation. So Mr. Raven says, "This is the way." Mr. Vane stubbornly replies, "I am quite content where I am." The wise Mr. Raven retorts, "You think so, but you are not. Come along." [1] Don't we sometimes sense we are perhaps too comfortable in a place where we don't really belong? Deep down we know that we need to be involved in an ongoing spiritual journey, but it's often hard to get started. We're seduced by the comfort of the familiar. But still the journey beckons.

In this book I've tried to tell some of my story. I've sought to tell of my own Cana-like crisis when I realized the wine had run out. I've tried to explain to those willing to read my story how I reached the point where I could no longer drink the grape juice of American consumer Christianity and call it wine. I've done my best to chronicle how Jesus did a miracle in my life by transforming watered-down pop Christianity into something glorious and intoxicating—the full-bodied wine of a deeper and richer faith. I suppose this is my apologia—my defense as to why I made such a radical and risky midlife course correction. To the many people (congregants, pastors, friends, readers, critics) who have asked, "Why did you do it?" this book is my answer. Of course, I really had no other choice. Once I'd found the good stuff of substantive theology, the Great Tradition, and historic Christianity, there was no going back. You can't unknow what you know and be true to yourself. But the changes I made were not merely for the sake of my own theological progress and spiritual wellbeing. I'm a pastor. I've been a pastor all of my adult life. God called me to preach the gospel, to lead people to faith in Jesus, to care for their souls. I "went public" with my new discoveries because I wanted to lead others into the beautiful Christianity I had found. I had to. I couldn't keep it to myself.

So this is some of my story. But to tell a story is to necessarily simplify what actually occurred. Our lives are so complex that we have to redact our telling of it or it could never be told. In telling my "water to wine" story I have emphasized the changes that began in 2004. That's one way of telling my story. To the outside observer that's when the visible changes in my theology and preaching began to be apparent. But that is only one way of telling this story. And while it's true enough, it's not entirely accurate; it's not the whole story. Until now I've left out a very important episode that happened four years earlier. This story needs to be told as well.

It was June 4, 2000, a beautiful Sunday afternoon in early summer. I was sitting on my front step reading Saint Augustine's *Confessions*. I hadn't yet begun to explore the Church Fathers, that would come four years later. But I was reading classic literature. By this time I had given up reading the trite little tomes of pop Christianity. I already knew what they said anyway. In a desire to read something of worth I had returned to the treasures of classic literature that I had first learned to love in Mrs. Zaft's high school literature class. I had read a fair number of the classics, but I had never read *Confessions*—the first, and perhaps greatest, spiritual autobiography in history. I had decided to read Augustine's *Confessions* for basically the same reason that I read Milton's *Paradise Lost* or Melville's *Moby Dick*—because it was an established classic in the canon of Western literature. And it is a remarkable book. The whole autobiography is a 350-page prayer. The book begins with this paragraph:

> You are great, Lord, and highly to be praised: Great is your power and your wisdom is immeasurable. Man, a little piece of your creation, desires to praise you, a human being bearing his mortality with him, carrying with him the witness of his sin and the witness that you resist the proud. Nevertheless, to praise you is the desire of

man, a little piece of your creation. You stir man
to take pleasure in praising you, because you have
made us for yourself, and our heart is restless until
it rests in you.[2]

"Our heart is restless until it rests in you." Those words
resonated with me. Sure, I was a Christian. But I was also a man
with a restless heart. A year earlier I had turned forty while
climbing Mount Kilimanjaro in Africa. Now I was beginning to
think about the second half of life…and I was restless. I had plenty
of success, but I was restless. I was still searching. And with the
clock ticking I feared I was running out of time. As I read
Confessions I learned of Augustine's life. A man my own age from
sixteen centuries earlier was telling me his story. He was the oldest
son of a pagan father and a Christian mother, raised among the
aristocracy of the late Roman Empire in North Africa. He told
unflinchingly of his somewhat profligate youth. He told of
teaching rhetoric in Milan and writing speeches for the emperor.
His genius was evident. He told in detail of his quest for truth in
the dualistic religion of Manichaeism and his eventual
disenchantment with it. He told of hearing the sermons of
Ambrose that pointed him in a new direction, of his longing to live
a moral life, and his despair at being incapable of it. He told
beautifully of his dramatic conversion on the day he heard a child's
voice singing in the garden, "Take and read," and how when he
turned at random in the New Testament he read Paul's words, "Put
on the Lord Jesus Christ" (Romans 13:14). He told of how he and
three other friends chose to enter a monastic life. He told of
becoming the bishop of Hippo. All along the way there were the

profound musings of a philosopher on the nature of time and memory, and more importantly, the prayers of a Christian seeker exploring the mysteries of God.

As I read *Confessions* on that Sunday afternoon, I was deeply moved. I closed the book, set it down beside me, and prayed this prayer, "O God, I want to dedicate the rest of my life to knowing you as you are revealed in Christ. As much as I can mean anything in a single moment, I mean this prayer. Help me to know you. Amen." As I finished my brief, but deeply honest prayer, something strange happened. I felt something in my chest. Words. I felt words, not in my mind, but in my chest—words I wanted to speak. I felt I had to say these words to someone, "Come with me. Come with me and you won't get cheated. Come with me." It was a mystical experience, an experience I couldn't deny or ignore.

So I started saying it to people, "Come with me." The following weekend I preached a sermon entitled "Come With Me." My text came from Paul's letter to the Colossians:

> As you therefore have received Christ Jesus the Lord, so walk in Him, rooted and built up in Him and established in the faith, as you have been taught, abounding in it with thanksgiving. Beware lest anyone cheat you through philosophy and empty deceit, according to the tradition of men, according to the basic principles of the world, and not according to Christ. For in Him dwells all the fullness of the Godhead bodily; and you are complete in Him, who is the head of all principality and power. (Colossians 2:6–10, NKJV)

These words from my sermon notes composed in June of 2000 will give you some idea of what I was preaching:

> Many Christians start out with Jesus but end up cheated. Instead of the endless adventure of searching out the mystery of Christ, they settle for something else. They get cheated. Come with me. I promise you won't get cheated. We're going to explore the fullness of Christ. Come with me.

That's what I was saying way back in 2000. I would return to my "come with me" theme over and over. I preached dozens of sermons along these lines, both when preaching at Word of Life and during my frequent travels. In churches, conferences, and youth events, I would preach my "Come With Me" sermon. I would dramatically tell the story of Augustine's conversion and of my mystical experience while reading *Confessions*. I would implore the audience, "Come with me. Let's explore the mystery of Christ. Come with me!" And I meant it. The only problem was that I didn't have the resources to search much beyond the limited confines of Charismatic Christian circles. I wanted to explore the mysteries of Christ, but most of what I knew came from the watered-down world of consumer Christianity. I was saying "Come with me," and sincerely trying to go somewhere, but I hadn't yet found the door to the wider world of richer Christianity. It would be four more years before Dallas Willard would kick open that door with his *Divine Conspiracy*. It wasn't until I learned to travel in the company of wise guides like Irenaeus, Athanasius, Gregory of Nyssa, Maximus the Confessor, St. Francis of Assisi, Julian of

Norwich, Søren Kierkegaard, George MacDonald, Karl Barth, Hans Urs von Balthasar, Abraham Joshua Heschel, Simone Weil, Thomas Merton, John Howard Yoder, René Girard, Frederick Buechner, Eugene Peterson, Walter Brueggemann, Wendell Berry, Kalistos Ware, Stanley Hauerwas, Richard Rohr, N.T. Wright, Scot McKnight, Miroslav Volf, David Bentley Hart, and so many others, that I learned to find my way well enough that "come with me" made any real sense. But once I had found the road to Cana, the place where Jesus was turning water into wine, I hit the road and didn't look back. Now "come with me" meant something. We were going somewhere!

What surprised me was that so many didn't join us in the journey. No doubt I was naïve. I suppose I should have known better, but it really did surprise me. And it hurt deeply. I honestly thought more would come with me than did. In time many new people did join us in the quest for a more authentic expression of the kingdom of Jesus, but so many who had been with us for years, people who were close friends, decided it was just too much change. It scared them. At a time when the culture wars were becoming more strident and divisive, a move toward greater ecumenism and a more generous attitude toward others was viewed with suspicion. So they left for places where they could cling to familiar themes. In retrospect I understand. I did what I had to do and they did what they had to do. Time heals all wounds, but the process can be very painful. The sad lesson I learned is that within Christian cultures that have confused faith with certitude, it's almost impossible for leaders to make any significant change, which means there is little or no freedom to really grow.

In his groundbreaking book, *Stages of Faith: The Psychology of Human Development and the Quest for Meaning*, James W. Fowler describes spiritual development in a series of stages, zero to six.

Fowler describes Stage Two as the faith of school children, a stage where metaphors are often literalized and a strong belief in the just reciprocity of the universe is held dear. At this stage of faith, the idea that good things happen to good people and bad things happen to bad people is a controlling axiom. Fowler describes Stage Five as the capacity to acknowledge paradox and experience transcendence. Fowler's final stage is characterized by compassion and the view that all people belong to a universal community. This is the mature stage where the spiritual journey breaks out of the paradigm of "us versus them" that dominates so much religious thought and so many religious institutions. Canadian theologian Brad Jersak, commenting on Fowler's stages of faith and the current plight of evangelicalism, makes this stinging observation:

> We desperately need more mature pastors who can lead their churches beyond dualism and dogmatism into contemplation and compassion.

> Entire streams of Christendom are not only stuck at stage-two faith, but actually train and require their ministers to interpret the Bible through the mythic-literal eyes of school children. Growing up and moving forward is rebranded as backsliding; maturing is perceived as falling away.[3]

If we are required to abide within a stage of spiritual development that believes giving right answers is the essence of spiritual maturity and that being good guarantees freedom from suffering, we are stuck in elementary school. We can preach the book of Proverbs, but not the book of Job; we can make sense of Deuteronomy, but not the Gospel of John. To become spiritually mature we have to recognize that suffering cannot be avoided and paradox is part of the program. But American consumer Christianity specializes in offering gimmicks that promise to eradicate suffering and theologies that claim to eliminate paradox. In our current religious and political climate, a following is most easily amassed by capitalizing on the polarizing approach that frames everything according to a dualistic "us versus them" paradigm. Sadly, this conspires to keep Christians immature and Christianity ugly. We have been rewarded for forming people according to the reactive life. Christian television and radio thrives on reactive ideologies. As Martin Laird says, "The reactive life is strengthened by these sudden spasms of talking, talking, talking, talking, to ourselves about life and love and how everybody ought to behave and vote."[4] We desperately need more mature pastors who can lead their churches beyond dualism and dogmatism into contemplation and compassion.

I became a pastor when I was twenty-two. (In reality I had been doing the work of a pastor since I was seventeen, but by the time I was twenty-two I had been ordained and embarked upon the fulltime vocation of being a pastor.) As I look back upon this, it does appear somewhat ridiculous. A twenty-two-year-old founding pastor! Do I regret it? Yes and no. I admit that it's probably not the best way to go about planting a church and making disciples, but it's what happened. It was part of the phenomenon of the Jesus Movement. Young would-be followers of Jesus were looking to me for leadership. It's the cards that were dealt me. So I did my best. I learned on the job. And the

Lord was with us. But by the time we began to have the success of numerical church growth in the 1990s, we were fully locked into the charismatic evangelicalism that too often appears committed to an elementary level of faith. Later I would discover just how difficult it can be to lead a large church beyond a quasi-fundamentalist and largely reactive Christianity. It's not impossible, but it's very difficult. And always painful.

Framing Christianity within a dualistic "us versus them" paradigm can be a successful way of achieving numerical growth. The nefarious "them" serve as a foil to assert our own rightness. Sunday after Sunday we are made to feel good about belonging to those who are on the right side of all things religious and political.

> We need the whole church to help us enter into the fullness of Christ.

This is the problem we have when churches are led by religious entrepreneurs instead of contemplative pastors. The other problem is that by the time a pastor is spiritually mature enough to actually be contemplative and capable of leading others into healthy spiritual formation, the institution is fully committed to a reactive kind of Christianity. If we are stuck in a reactive form of Christianity, any move toward a contemplative form of Christianity is viewed as a kind of betrayal. It's often condemned as "falling away from the faith." But that's not what it is. It's leaving behind childish things and growing up into the fullness of Christ.

The problem of the American evangelical church being led primarily by those who are committed to a reactive form of Christianity is widespread. It's why so few of our best known pastors look anything like contemplative mystics. Yet contemplative mystics are precisely the kind of women and men that need to be leading our churches. More so now than ever. We're in a situation where it is often very difficult, if not impossible, for a pastor to make spiritual progress *while being a pastor*. I know, because I talk to these pastors all the time. Being familiar with my story, they seek me out. Many of them feel they have to make a choice between their own spiritual growth and their pastoral vocation. Something needs to change. As long as our churches are led by those who view being a Christian primarily as a kind of conferred status instead of a lifelong journey, and view faith as a form of static certitude instead of an ongoing orientation of the soul toward God, I see little hope that we can build the kind of churches that can produce mature believers in any significant numbers.

The American entrepreneurial model of church growth has created a situation where the pastoral vocation has been rendered nearly impossible. On one hand the pastor must satisfy the demands of a consumer-oriented constituency (which is more properly the work of a politician or businessman), while on the other hand seeking to produce real spiritual formation in the lives of the congregation. These two objectives—satisfying a contingency and spiritual formation—work against one another most of the time. It seems impossible. But Jesus calls us to do the impossible. So we press on…in faith. Our hearts are not weary. We still say, "come with me." We still seek to lead people into the fullness of Christ. Because it is Jesus who calls us and it is Jesus who is building his church. There are those who are longing to walk the road to Cana and find the place where water is turned into wine.

In November of 2013 Peri and I hiked the Jesus Trail in Israel. Over a period of four days we walked forty-two miles from Nazareth to Capernaum—from Jesus' hometown in the Galilean hills to the seaside town where Jesus lived during his ministry years. It was one of the most memorable and enjoyable things we have ever done. On the first day, our trek took us from Nazareth to Cana, beginning at the Basilica of the Annunciation in the center of Nazareth. After finding our way out of the modern city of Nazareth, we began to hike on dusty roads and faint trails beside endless olive groves. We passed through Arab villages and Jewish *kibbutzim*. When we arrived at Cana, it seemed like every other shop was selling wine. Of course. Jesus' first miracle assured that Cana would forever be associated with wine. We stayed in the home of a delightful Arab Christian couple. They were Greek Orthodox and quite hospitable. Their living room was adorned with beautiful Orthodox icons—especially icons depicting the miracle that has made their little town famous wherever the gospel is proclaimed. They were obviously proud to live in the town where Jesus had performed his first miracle.

Our hosts' house was next door to a mosque. It was a warm night and we slept with the windows open. At 4:30 in the morning we were awakened by the amplified call to prayer coming from the mosque next door. The loudspeaker on the mosque's minaret was near our window. It was deafening! At breakfast I asked our host if he had gotten used to the predawn call to prayer, if he had learned to sleep through it? "No," he said, and I asked, "Then what do you do?" He smiled, shrugged his shoulders and said, "I pray." Which is what I had done that morning. Unable to go back to sleep, I prayed; as I prayed I contemplated how each branch of Christianity has its own unique emphasis on Christ. The Orthodox give us the Christ of Glory. The Orthodox have their beautiful icons and a high Christology. The Catholics give us the Suffering

Christ, which is why the crucifix is so prominent in Catholicism. The Anglicans give us Christ the Teacher—so many of our best theologians either come from the Anglicans or eventually find their home there. Protestants give us the Reforming Christ, the Jesus who challenges the Pharisees and cleanses the Temple. Evangelicals give us the Personal Jesus, the Jesus who calls his disciples by name and talks to Nicodemus about being born again. Pentecostals give us the miracle-working Jesus, who heals the sick and casts out demons.

Of course, each of these emphases have their own potential pitfalls. The Orthodox with their high Christology can lose sight of the humanity of Christ. Catholics can become morbid in their focus on the suffering Christ. Anglicans can become too academic in their understanding of Christ. Protestants can become too divisive in their effort to follow the reforming Christ. The Evangelical emphasis on a personal relationship with Jesus can erode into private sentimentality. The Pentecostal emphasis on the miracles of Jesus can lead to an unhealthy obsession with the sensational. The safeguard is obvious. We need the whole church to help us enter into the fullness of Christ. This was my meditation after our Muslim neighbors had faithfully awakened me for prayer. These were the kind of thoughts that would have been impossible at an earlier stage of my spiritual journey. I had been too committed to tribalism. I had to believe that my tribe had it all and that the other tribes needed to join my tribe so we could all be alike. Unity was to be achieved through a bland sameness. But once I began to sip some of the wine that Jesus was offering, I began to see things differently. Christianity is a symposium, a symphony, and we need our beautiful diversity.

After a hearty breakfast with our delightful hosts in Cana, we were out the door and back on the Jesus Trail. We would pass through towns and villages, forests and farms, olive groves and citrus orchards. We would lose our way now and then, and then pick up the discreet painted blazes that marked the trail. We crossed streams in deep valleys and hiked to the top of the Horns of Hattin. When we arrived at a Jewish *kibbutz* on the Sabbath, famished from our journey, there was nothing to eat. So they kindly directed us to an Arab restaurant down the road that happily served us savory kabobs. On the last day we scrambled down the steep cliffs of Mount Arbel and hiked past the Mount of Beatitudes framed by a rainbow. It was perfect. We went into the ancient church at Tabgha to see the fourth-century mosaic commemorating Jesus' miracle of the loaves and fishes. We cooled our weary feet in the Sea of Galilee. At dusk we reached our destination at Capernaum. The pilgrim tours had left and we had the ancient synagogue to ourselves. I pulled my Book of Common Prayer out of my dusty backpack and prayed the evening office. A friend who is a Catholic priest had asked me to pray for him when I was in the Capernaum synagogue where Jesus had taught. So I did. Finally we called for a taxi to pick us up and take us to a hotel in Tiberius. When the taxi arrived and we got in, a Bob Dylan song was playing:

> One more cup of coffee for the road
> One more cup of coffee 'fore I go
> To the valley below
> —Bob Dylan, "One More Cup Of Coffee (Valley Below)"

It was the perfect end to our journey on the Jesus Trail.

I've thought often about those four days on the Jesus Trail. It's an apt metaphor for what the Christian life is really like. It's not static. It's not standing still. It's not sitting in the same pew for fifty years. It's not grimly holding onto the same doctrinaire attitudes you held when you lived by the lies that life is black and white. The Christian life is a journey. It's a road. We have to walk it. Jesus' call to discipleship is always the same—"Follow me." It's presumed that we are going to be on the move. We're going somewhere. The Christian life really is following in the ancient footsteps of Jesus through a modern world. We have to find our way by looking for the subtle blazes that mark the way. On the Jesus Trail we did lose our way a time or two, forcing us to retrace our steps and find out where we'd gone wrong. But that's exactly what it's like walking the Jesus way through life. We make mistakes. We correct our mistakes. We press on.

> The Christian life really is following in the ancient footsteps of Jesus through a modern world.

If the journey has its proper effect, we learn to let go of our fears and walk through life as open souls. We meet all kinds of people along life's journey, like we did on the Jesus Trail. Christians of every stripe. Jews and Muslims. Palestinians and Israelis. Believers and unbelievers. If we have the common ground of a shared faith, that's wonderful. If not, we enjoy the common ground of our shared humanity. There's always common ground if we are willing to find it. If we stay on the road following the Jesus way, what we discover is that we are walking farther and farther down the road of love. We learn to be open and generous. We learn to love everyone we meet. To accept them. To include them. To recognize that they too are children of

God. This is the beauty of learning openness on the open road of life.

O To Be Open
O to be open
It's what the wise ones seek
It's what the great souls attain

What's a saint?
An Open One
Saint Francis and Mother Teresa were
Open
Open to God, open to Creation, open to the Other
We're all born open—wide-eyed and wide open
What's an infant?
An Open One
Wonder, learning, and love come easy to a
Child

But then we suffer the blows
And begin to
Close

By the time we're a teen
We're mostly tight shut
Happy or sad
A clam inside a shell

Now the task begins

The task of a lifetime
The task of becoming
Open
O to be open
An old one open again
Open to wonder, learning, and love
To grow open is to grow young

Much is against openness
Vested interests stake much on keeping us
Tight shut
The talking heads of the tight shut tell us of
Right and Wrong, Black and White, Us and Them
Who is In and who is Out
Their words are a slamming door
BAM!
Tight shut!
To live in the world of the tight shut is called
Certainty and security, clarity and conformity
It's also death
To live there is to shrivel your soul
To die there is—
Well, I don't know

I do know that to save my soul
I must become open
Open to God's all-encompassing love
I cannot afford to slam the door
To shut the door on "them"

Is to lock myself in hell's closet

O to be open
Where does the first crack of openness come from?
It could come from anywhere
A poem, a heartbreak, a sunset really seen
A song, a sermon, a mercy freely received
A birth, a death, a person fully loved
Let openness get its foot in the door
And it'll begin to shovel the grace in

Open to the openness
The openness of God
The openness of light
The openness of love

Life is open
(Ever unfolding)
Death is closed
(A sealed tomb)

Heaven is open
(Its gates will never be shut)
Hell is closed
(Abandon all hope ye who enter)
Jesus is the Usher of Openness
He holds the keys of Hell and Death
To set its prisoners free
May he loose us and lead us into

The Great Openness of God

O to be open

The paradox is that the narrow way leads to broad acceptance. The narrow way is not narrow-mindedness. The narrow way is exactly what Jesus said it is—treating others with the generosity of love. The golden rule is the narrow gate.

> In everything do to others as you would have them do to you; for this is the law and the prophets. Enter through the narrow gate... (Matthew 7:12–13)

There is a road that leads to Cana. The place where the miracles begin. The place where Jesus turns water into wine. There is a kind of Christianity that looks like a wedding feast. It's why I still say "come with me." I want you to find the beautiful faith that lies beyond the cruel confines of fundamentalist fears and political agendas. I want you to find the generous orthodoxy that transcends tribalism. I want you to find the sacred mystery that is far deeper than shallow certitude. I want to say, "Come with me, come to Cana, come to where Jesus turns water into wine."

L'Chaim!
Water turned to wine
The miracle is the time
That it did not take
For common to turn extraordinaire

Tap water into carménère
Drawn from pots of ritual purity
Taken to the master of the party
Hints of plum and kingdom come
Salute!

In Nazareth he was called the carpenter
In Cana he became a master vintner
Sommelier said it's a hundred point wine
The miracle-worker did it without a vine
A whole barrel of vintage year thirty
Better than the best from Cape Verde
All so the feast would not cease
A toast to Mary for her idea
L'chaim!

We walked from Nazareth to Cana
In the fall of my fifty-fourth year
Talking Jesus all along the way
Took us the better part of a day
Every other store up and down the line
A Christian selling some kind of wine
Call it a entrepreneurial witness to—
Jesus' first miracle
Cheers!

Water turned to wine
The mystery is the time
It takes for my own transformation

A slow and painful fermentation
With a soul like crushed grapes
I'm a dusty bottle in God's cellar
But the winemaker knows his craft
He makes all things beautiful in their time
Hallelujah!

Water To Wine Playlist

This playlist is the soundtrack for *Water To Wine*. Many of the songs are referred to in the book, some of the songs have obvious connections with certain passages, and a few of the songs have a deeply personal connection with the story I tell. You can listen to this playlist online at www.watertowinebook.com.

The Pretender – Foo Fighters
I Still Haven't Found What I'm Looking For – U2
Ballad Of A Thin Man – Bob Dylan
Change In The Wind – Paul Clark
X-Files Theme – DJ Dado
Changing Of The Guards – Bob Dylan
Revolution – The Beatles
Shot Down – Larry Norman
It's Alright Ma (I'm Only Bleeding) – Bob Dylan
Jesus, Etc. – Wilco
Poverty – Jason Upton
Sweetheart Like You – Bob Dylan
Imagine – John Lennon
Viva la Vida – Coldplay
Ring Them Bells – Bob Dylan
Peace Train – Cat Stevens
The Passenger – Iggy Pop

All Along The Watchtower – Bob Dylan

Instant Karma – John Lennon

If A Tree Falls – Bruce Cockburn

Between The Graveyard And The Garden – Jason Upton

Acknowledgement (A Love Supreme) – John Coltrane

One More Cup Of Coffee – Bob Dylan

Time – Pink Floyd

Truckin' – Grateful Dead

Every Grain Of Sand – Bob Dylan

Resurrection Fern – Iron & Wine

Wake Up – Arcade Fire

Water Into Wine – Bruce Cockburn

Home – Foo Fighters

Endnotes

Chapter 1: Twenty-Two Days

[1] Luke 5:39, *Message Bible*

[2] Terry Theise, *Reading Between the Wines* (Oakland, CA: University of California Press, 2011), 54.

[3] Henri J.M. Nouwen, *Can You Drink This Cup?* (South Bend, IN: Ave Maria Press, 2006), 54.

[4] J.R.R. Tolkien, *The Fellowship of the Ring: Being the First Part of The Lord of the Rings* (Boston, MA: Mariner Books, 2012), 32.

[5] Richard Foster, forward to *The Divine Conspiracy*, by Dallas Willard (San Francisco, CA: HarperCollins, 1997), ix.

[6] Eugene Peterson, *Christ Plays In Ten Thousand Places* (Grand Rapids, MI: Eerdmans, 2005), 125.

[7] George MacDonald, *The Curate's Awakening* (Bloomington, MN: Bethany House, 1985), 217.

[8] Frederick Buechner, *The Alphabet of Grace* (San Francisco, CA: HarperCollins, 2009), 47.

[9] Søren Kierkegaard, *Provocations: Spiritual Writings of Kierkegaard* (Maryknoll, NY: Obis Books, 2004), 3.

Chapter 2: Five Words

[1] John Behr, *Becoming Human* (Yonkers, NY: St Vladimir's Seminary Press, 2013), 108-109.

[2] Thomas Merton, *Conjectures of a Guilty Bystander* (Colorado Springs, CO: Image Books, 1968), 14.

[3] Eugene Peterson, *Reversed Thunder* (San Francisco, NY: HarperCollins 1988), 117.

Chapter 3: Three Dreams
[1] Bob Dylan, *Chronicles* (New York: Simon & Schuster, 2005), 35.
[2] Richard Rohr, *Radical Grace: Daily Meditations* (Cincinnati, OH: St. Anthony Messenger Press, 1995), 173.

Chapter 4: Jerusalem Bells
[1] "Richard Rohr's Daily Mediation," August 22, 2013 <http://myemail.constantcontact.com/Richard-Rohr-s-Daily-Meditation----August-22--2013.html?soid=1103098668616&aid=zvilJQMRT_0> Last accessed October 21, 2015.
[2] Kurt Vonnegut as quoted by Eugene Peterson, *Tell It Slant* (Grand Rapids, MI: Eerdmans, 2008), 188.

Chapter 5: Sitting with Jesus
[1] Julian of Norwich, *Revelations of Divine Love (Short Text and Long Text)*, translated by Elizabeth Spearing, (New York: Penguin Books, 1999), 177.

Chapter 6: Echoes, Silence, Patience & Grace
[1] Brian Zahnd, *What To Do On the Worst Day of Your Life* (Lake Mary, FL: Christian Life, 2009), xiv, xv.
[2] G.K. Chesterton, *Saint Francis of Assisi* (EMP Books, 2012), 122.
[3] St. John of the Cross, *Dark Night of the Soul* (New York: Dover Publications, 2012), 104.
[4] Julian of Norwich, *Revelations of Divine Love*, 85.
[5] G.K. Chesterton, *Orthodoxy* (Ortho Publishing, 2014), 41.
[6] Yves Congar as quoted by Hans Boersma, *Nouvelle Theologie and Sacramental Ontology: A Return to Mystery* (New York: Oxford University Press, 2009), 1.
[7] Eugene Peterson, *A Long Obedience in the Same Direction: Discipleship in an Instant Society* (Downers Grove, IL: IVP Books, 2000), 17.
[8] Stanley Hauerwas, *Hannah's Child: A Theologian's Memoir* (Grand Rapids, MI: Eerdmans, 2010), 274.

Chapter 7: Grain and Grape

[1] Brian Zahnd, *A Farewell To Mars* (Colorado Springs, CO: David C. Cook, 2014).

[2] Karl Rahner, *Theological Investigations 7* (London: Darton, Longman & Todd, 1971), 15.

[3] Annie Dillard, *Holy the Firm* (New York: HarperCollins, 1977), 63–64.

[4] *Book of Common Prayer*, Collect for Wednesday in Easter Week

Chapter 8: Every Grain of Sand

[1] Wendell Berry, *The Art of the Commonplace: The Agrarian Essays of Wendell Berry* (Berkeley, CA: Counterpoint, 2003), 311.

[2] James Welch, *Winter in the Blood* (New York: Penguin Books, 2008), 54-55.

[3] T.S. Eliot, *Christianity and Culture* (Boston, MA: Mariner Books, 1977), 49.

[4] Fyodor Dostoevsky, *The Brothers Karamazov*, translated by Richard Pevear and Larissa Volokhonsky (San Francisco: North Point Press, 1990), 319.

[5] Ludwig Wittgenstein, *Tractatus Logico-Philosophicus*, 471st edition (New York: Dover Publications, 1998), 89.

[6] Dostoevsky, *The Brothers Karamazov*, 322.

[7] Ibid., 323.

[8] *Nicene and Post-Nicene Fathers* Vol. 7, edited by Philip Schaff (Peabody, MA: Hendrikson Publishers,1999), 504.

Chapter 9: Come With Me

[1] George MacDonald, *Lilith* (Doylestown, PA: Wildside Press, 2002), 20.

[2] Saint Augustine, *Confessions* (New York: Oxford University Press, 2009), 3.

[3] Brad Jersak, *A More Christlike God* (Pasadena, CA: Plain Truth Ministries, 2015), 141.

[4] Martin Laird, *A Sunlit Absence* (New York: Oxford University Press, 2011), 18.

79 W/p + liturgy

Printed in Great Britain
by Amazon